INTERNATIONAL FINANCIAL STATEMENT ANALYSIS WORKBOOK

CFA Institute is the premier association for investment professionals around the world, with over 95,000 members in 134 countries. Since 1963 the organization has developed and administered the renowned Chartered Financial Analyst® Program. With a rich history of leading the investment profession, CFA Institute has set the highest standards in ethics, education, and professional excellence within the global investment community, and is the foremost authority on investment profession conduct and practice.

Each book in the CFA Institute Investment Series is geared toward industry practitioners, along with graduate-level finance students, and covers the most important topics in the industry. The authors of these cutting-edge books are themselves industry professionals and academics and bring their wealth of knowledge and expertise to this series.

INTERNATIONAL FINANCIAL STATEMENT ANALYSIS WORKBOOK

Thomas R. Robinson, CFA

Hennie van Greuning, CFA

Elaine Henry, CFA

Michael A. Broihahn, CFA

WILEY

John Wiley & Sons, Inc.

For general information on our other products and services or for technical support, please contact our Customer Care Department within the United States at (800) 762-2974, outside the United States at (317) 572-3993 or fax (317) 572-4002.

Wiley also publishes its books in a variety of electronic formats. Some content that appears in print may not be available in electronic books. For more information about Wiley products, visit our web site at www.wiley.com.

ISBN-13 978-0-470-28767-5

Printed in the United States of America

10 9 8 7 6 5 4 3 2 1

CONTENTS

CHAPTER 6
Understanding the Cash Flow Statement

CHAPTER 7
Financial Analysis Techniques

CHAPTER 8
International Standards Convergence

CHAPTER 9
Financial Statement Analysis: Applications

CHAPTER 10
Inventories

CHAPTER 11
Long-Lived Assets

CHAPTER 12
Income Taxes

INTERNATIONAL FINANCIAL STATEMENT ANALYSIS WORKBOOK

PART I

LEARNING OUTCOMES, SUMMARY OVERVIEW, AND PROBLEMS

CHAPTER 1

FINANCIAL STATEMENT ANALYSIS: AN INTRODUCTION

Thomas R. Robinson, CFA

CFA Institute
Charlottesville, Virginia

Hennie van Greuning, CFA

World Bank
Washington, DC

Elaine Henry, CFA

University of Miami
Miami, Florida

Michael A. Broihahn, CFA

Barry University
Miami, Florida

LEARNING OUTCOMES

After completing this chapter, you will be able to do the following:

- Discuss the roles of financial reporting and financial statement analysis.
- Discuss the roles of the key financial statements (income statement, balance sheet, cash flow statement, and statement of changes in owners' equity) in evaluating a company's performance and financial position.

- Discuss the importance of financial statement notes and supplementary information (including disclosures of accounting methods, estimates, and assumptions) and management's discussion and analysis.
- Discuss the objective of audits of financial statements, the types of audit reports, and the importance of effective internal controls.
- Identify and explain information sources besides annual financial statements and supplementary information that analysts use in financial statement analysis.
- Describe the steps in the financial statement analysis framework.

SUMMARY OVERVIEW

This chapter has presented an overview of financial statement analysis. Among the major points covered are the following:

- The primary purpose of financial reports is to provide information and data about a company's financial position and performance, including profitability and cash flows. The information presented in financial reports—including the financial statements, financial notes, and management's discussion and analysis—allows the financial analyst to assess a company's financial position and performance and trends in that performance.
- Key financial statements that are a primary focus of analysis include the income statement, balance sheet, cash flow statement, and statement of owners' equity.
- The income statement presents information on the financial results of a company's business activities over a period of time. The income statement communicates how much revenue the company generated during a period and what costs it incurred in connection with generating that revenue. The basic equation underlying the income statement is Revenue − Expense = Net income.
- The balance sheet discloses what a company owns (assets) and what it owes (liabilities) at a specific point in time. Owners' equity represents the portion belonging to the owners or shareholders of the business; it is the residual interest in the assets of an entity after deducting its liabilities. The three parts of the balance sheet are formulated in the accounting relationship of Assets = Liabilities + Owners' equity.
- Although the income statement and balance sheet provide a measure of a company's success, cash and cash flow are also vital to a company's long-term success. Disclosing the sources and uses of cash in the cash flow statement helps creditors, investors, and other statement users evaluate the company's liquidity, solvency, and financial flexibility.
- The statement of changes in owners' equity reflects information about the increases or decreases to a company's owners' equity.
- In addition to the financial statements, a company provides other sources of financial information that are useful to the financial analyst. As part of his or her analysis, the financial analyst should read and assess the information presented in the company's financial note disclosures and supplementary schedules as well as the information contained in the MD&A. Analysts must also evaluate footnote disclosures regarding the use of alternative accounting methods, estimates, and assumptions.
- A publicly traded company must have an independent audit performed on its year-end financial statements. The auditor's opinion provides some assurance about whether the

financial statements fairly reflect a company's performance and financial position. In addition, for U.S. publicly traded companies, management must demonstrate that the company's internal controls are effective.

- The financial statement analysis framework provides steps that can be followed in any financial statement analysis project, including the following:
  - ○ Articulate the purpose and context of the analysis.
  - ○ Collect input data.
  - ○ Process data.
  - ○ Analyze/interpret the processed data.
  - ○ Develop and communicate conclusions and recommendations.
  - ○ Follow up.

PROBLEMS

1. Providing information about the performance and financial position of companies so that users can make economic decisions *best* describes the role of
   A. auditing.
   B. financial reporting.
   C. financial statement analysis.

2. A company's current financial position would *best* be evaluated using the
   A. balance sheet.
   B. income statement.
   C. cash flow statement.

3. A company's profitability for a period would *best* be evaluated using the
   A. balance sheet.
   B. income statement.
   C. cash flow statement.

4. Accounting methods, estimates, and assumptions used in preparing financial statements are found
   A. in footnotes.
   B. in the auditor's report.
   C. in the proxy statement.

5. Information about management and director compensation would *best* be found
   A. in footnotes.
   B. in the auditor's report.
   C. in the proxy statement.

6. Information about material events and uncertainties would *best* be found in
   A. footnotes.
   B. the proxy statement.
   C. management's discussion and analysis.

7. What type of audit opinion is preferred when analyzing financial statements?
   A. Qualified.
   B. Adverse.
   C. Unqualified.

8. Ratios are an input into which step in the financial analysis framework?
   A. Process data.
   B. Collect input data.
   C. Analyze/interpret the processed data.

CHAPTER 2

FINANCIAL REPORTING MECHANICS

Thomas R. Robinson, CFA

CFA Institute
Charlottesville, Virginia

Hennie van Greuning, CFA

World Bank
Washington, DC

Elaine Henry, CFA

University of Miami
Miami, Florida

Michael A. Broihahn, CFA

Barry University
Miami, Florida

LEARNING OUTCOMES

After completing this chapter, you will be able to do the following:

- Identify the groups (operating, investing, and financing activities) into which business activities are categorized for financial reporting purposes and classify any business activity in the appropriate group.
- Explain the relationship of financial statement elements and accounts, and classify accounts into the financial statement elements.

- Explain the accounting equation in its basic and expanded forms.
- Explain the process of recording business transactions using an accounting system based on the accounting equations.
- Explain the need for accruals and other adjustments in preparing financial statements.
- Prepare financial statements given account balances and/or other elements in the relevant accounting equation, and explain the relationships among the income statement, balance sheet, statement of cash flows, and statement of owners' equity.
- Describe the flow of information in an accounting system.
- Explain the use of the results of the accounting process in security analysis.

SUMMARY OVERVIEW

The accounting process is a key component of financial reporting. The mechanics of this process convert business transactions into records necessary to create periodic reports on a company. An understanding of these mechanics is useful in evaluating financial statements for credit and equity analysis purposes and in forecasting future financial statements. Key concepts are as follows:

- Business activities can be classified into three groups: operating activities, investing activities, and financing activities.
- Companies classify transactions into common accounts that are components of the five financial statement elements: assets, liabilities, equity, revenue, and expense.
- The core of the accounting process is the basic accounting equation: Assets = Liabilities + Owners' equity.
- The expanded accounting equation is Assets = Liabilities + Contributed capital + Beginning retained earnings + Revenue − Expenses − Dividends.
- Business transactions are recorded in an accounting system that is based on the basic and expanded accounting equations.
- The accounting system tracks and summarizes data used to create financial statements: the balance sheet, income statement, statement of cash flows, and statement of owners' equity. The statement of retained earnings is a component of the statement of owners' equity.
- Accruals are a necessary part of the accounting process and are designed to allocate activity to the proper period for financial reporting purposes.
- The results of the accounting process are financial reports that are used by managers, investors, creditors, analysts, and others in making business decisions.
- An analyst uses the financial statements to make judgments on the financial health of a company.
- Company management can manipulate financial statements, and a perceptive analyst can use his or her understanding of financial statements to detect misrepresentations.

PROBLEMS

1. Which of the following items would most likely be classified as an operating activity?
   A. Issuance of debt
   B. Acquisition of a competitor
   C. Sale of automobiles by an automobile dealer

2. Which of the following items would most likely be classified as a financing activity?
   A. Issuance of debt
   B. Payment of income taxes
   C. Investments in the stock of a supplier

3. Which of the following elements represents an economic resource?
   A. Asset
   B. Liability
   C. Owners' equity

4. Which of the following elements represents a residual claim?
   A. Asset
   B. Liability
   C. Owners' equity

5. An analyst has projected that a company will have assets of €2,000 at year-end and liabilities of €1,200. The analyst's projection of total owners' equity should be closest to
   A. €800.
   B. €2,000.
   C. €3,200.

6. An analyst has collected the following information regarding a company in advance of its year-end earnings announcement (in millions):

Estimated net income	$200
Beginning retained earnings	$1,400
Estimated distributions to owners	$100

   The analyst's estimate of ending retained earnings (in millions) should be closest to
   A. $1,300.
   B. $1,500.
   C. $1,700.

7. An analyst has compiled the following information regarding Rubsam, Inc.

Liabilities at year-end	€1,000
Contributed capital at year-end	€500
Beginning retained earnings	€600
Revenue during the year	€5,000
Expenses during the year	€4,300

   There have been no distributions to owners. The analyst's most likely estimate of total assets at year-end should be closest to
   A. €2,100.
   B. €2,300.
   C. €2,800.

8. A group of individuals formed a new company with an investment of $500,000. The most likely effect of this transaction on the company's accounting equation at the time of the formation is an increase in cash and
   A. an increase in revenue.
   B. an increase in liabilities.
   C. an increase in contributed capital.

9. HVG, LLC paid $12,000 of cash to a real estate company upon signing a lease on 31 December 2005. The payment represents a $4,000 security deposit and $4,000 of rent for each of January 2006 and February 2006. Assuming that the correct accounting is to reflect both January and February rent as prepaid, the most likely effect on HVG's accounting equation in December 2005 is
   A. no net change in assets.
   B. a decrease in assets of $8,000.
   C. a decrease in assets of $12,000.

10. TRR Enterprises sold products to customers on 30 June 2006 for a total price of €10,000. The terms of the sale are that payment is due in 30 days. The cost of the products was €8,000. The most likely net change in TRR's total assets on 30 June 2006 related to this transaction is
   A. €0.
   B. €2,000.
   C. €10,000.

11. On 30 April 2006, Pinto Products received a cash payment of $30,000 as a deposit on production of a custom machine to be delivered in August 2006. This transaction would most likely result in which of the following on 30 April 2006?
   A. No effect on liabilities
   B. A decrease in assets of $30,000
   C. An increase in liabilities of $30,000

12. Squires & Johnson, Ltd., recorded €250,000 of depreciation expense in December 2005. The most likely effect on the company's accounting equation is
   A. no effect on assets.
   B. a decrease in assets of €250,000.
   C. an increase in liabilities of €250,000.

13. An analyst who is interested in assessing a company's financial position is most likely to focus on which financial statement?
   A. Balance sheet
   B. Income statement
   C. Statement of cash flows

14. The statement of cash flows presents the flows into which three groups of business activities?
   A. Operating, nonoperating, and financing
   B. Operating, investing, and financing
   C. Operating, nonoperating, and investing

15. Which of the following statements about cash received prior to the recognition of revenue in the financial statements is *most* accurate? The cash is recorded as
   A. deferred revenue, an asset.
   B. accrued revenue, a liability.
   C. deferred revenue, a liability.

16. When, at the end of an accounting period, a revenue has been recognized in the financial statements but no billing has occurred and no cash has been received, the accrual is to
    A. unbilled (accrued) revenue, an asset.
    B. deferred revenue, an asset.
    C. unbilled (accrued) revenue, a liability.

17. When, at the end of an accounting period, cash has been paid with respect to an expense incurred but not yet recognized in the financial statements, the business should then record
    A. an accrued expense, an asset.
    B. a prepaid expense, an asset.
    C. an accrued expense, a liability.

18. When, at the end of an accounting period, cash has not been paid with respect to an expense that has been incurred but not recognized yet in the financial statements, the business should then record
    A. an accrued expense, an asset.
    B. a prepaid expense, an asset.
    C. an accrued expense, a liability.

19. The collection of all business transactions sorted by account in an accounting system is referred to as
    A. a trial balance.
    B. a general ledger.
    C. a general journal.

20. If a company reported fictitious revenue, it could try to cover up its fraud by
    A. decreasing assets.
    B. increasing liabilities.
    C. creating a fictitious asset.

CHAPTER 3

FINANCIAL REPORTING STANDARDS

Thomas R. Robinson, CFA

CFA Institute
Charlottesville, Virginia

Hennie van Greuning, CFA

World Bank
Washington, DC

Elaine Henry, CFA

University of Miami
Miami, Florida

Michael A. Broihahn, CFA

Barry University
Miami, Florida

LEARNING OUTCOMES

After completing this chapter, you will be able to do the following:

- Explain the objective of financial statements and the importance of reporting standards in security analysis and valuation.
- Explain the role of financial reporting standard-setting bodies (including the International Accounting Standards Board and the U.S. Financial Accounting Standards Board) and

regulatory authorities such as the International Organization of Securities Commissions, the U.K. Financial Services Authority, and the U.S. Securities and Exchange Commission in establishing and enforcing reporting standards.
- Discuss the status of global convergence of accounting standards and the ongoing barriers to developing one universally accepted set of financial reporting standards.
- Describe the International Financial Reporting Standards (IFRS) framework, including the objective of financial statements, their qualitative characteristics, required reporting elements, and the constraints and assumptions in preparing financial statements.
- Explain the general requirements for financial statements.
- Compare and contrast the key concepts of financial reporting standards under IFRS and alternative reporting systems, and discuss the implications for financial analysis of differing financial reporting systems.
- Identify the characteristics of a coherent financial reporting framework and barriers to creating such a framework.
- Discuss the importance of monitoring developments in financial reporting standards and evaluate company disclosures of significant accounting policies.

SUMMARY OVERVIEW

An awareness of the reporting framework underlying financial reports can assist in security valuation and other financial analysis. The framework describes the objectives of financial reporting, desirable characteristics for financial reports, the elements of financial reports, and the underlying assumptions and constraints of financial reporting. An understanding of the framework, broader than knowledge of a particular set of rules, offers an analyst a basis from which to infer the proper financial reporting, and thus security valuation implications, of *any* financial statement element or transaction.

We have discussed how financial reporting systems are developed, the conceptual objectives of financial reporting standards, the parties involved in standard-setting processes, and how financial reporting standards are converging into one global set of standards. A summary of the key points for each section is noted below:

- *The objective of financial reporting:*
  - The objective of financial statements is to provide information about the financial position, performance, and changes in financial position of an entity; this information should be useful to a wide range of users for the purpose of making economic decisions.[1]
  - Financial reporting requires policy choices and estimates. These choices and estimates require judgment, which can vary from one preparer to the next. Accordingly, standards are needed to attempt to ensure some type of consistency in these judgments.
- *Financial reporting standard-setting bodies and regulatory authorities.* Private sector standard-setting bodies and regulatory authorities play significant but different roles in the standard-setting process. In general, standard-setting bodies make the rules, and regulatory authorities enforce the rules. However, regulators typically retain legal authority to establish financial reporting standards in their jurisdiction.

---

[1]*Framework for the Preparation and Presentation of Financial Statements,* IASC, 1989, adopted by IASB 2001, paragraph 12.

- *Convergence of global financial reporting standards.* The IASB and FASB, along with other standard setters, are working to achieve convergence of financial reporting standards. Listed companies in many countries are adopting IFRS. Barriers to full convergence still exist.
- *The IFRS Framework.* The IFRS Framework sets forth the concepts that underlie the preparation and presentation of financial statements for external users, provides further guidance on the elements from which financial statements are constructed, and discusses concepts of capital and capital maintenance.
  - The objective of fair presentation of useful information is the center of the Framework. The qualitative characteristics of useful information include understandability, relevance, reliability, and comparability.
  - The IFRS Framework identifies the following elements of financial statements: assets, liabilities, equity, income, expense, and capital maintenance adjustments.
  - The Framework is constructed based on the underlying assumptions of accrual basis and going concern but acknowledges three inherent constraints: timeliness, benefit versus cost, and balance between qualitative characteristics.
- *IFRS financial statements.* IAS No. 1 prescribes that a complete set of financial statements includes a balance sheet, an income statement, a statement of changes in equity, a cash flow statement, and notes. The notes include a summary of significant accounting policies and other explanatory information.
  - Financial statements need to adhere to the fundamental principles of fair presentation, going concern, accrual basis, consistency, and materiality.
  - Financial statements must also satisfy the presentation requirements of appropriate aggregation, no offsetting, and a classified balance sheet. Statements must provide the required minimum information on the face of the financial statements and note disclosures.
- *Comparison with alternative reporting systems.* A significant number of the world's listed companies report under either IFRS or U.S. GAAP. Although these standards are moving toward convergence, there are still significant differences in the framework and individual standards. Frequently, companies provide reconciliations and disclosures regarding the significant differences between reporting bases. These reconciliations can be reviewed to identify significant items that could affect security valuation.
- *Characteristics of a coherent financial reporting framework.* Effective frameworks share three characteristics: transparency, comprehensiveness, and consistency. Effective standards can, however, have conflicting approaches on valuation, the bases for standard setting (principle or rules based), and resolution of conflicts between balance sheet and income statement focus.
- *Monitoring developments.* Analysts can remain aware of ongoing developments in financial reporting by monitoring three areas: new products or transactions, standard setters' and regulators' actions, and company disclosures regarding critical accounting policies and estimates.

PROBLEMS

1. Which of the following is not an objective of financial statements as expressed by the International Accounting Standards Board?
   A. To provide information about the performance of an entity
   B. To provide information about the financial position of an entity
   C. To provide information about the users of an entity's financial statements

2. International accounting standards are currently developed by which entity?
   A. Financial Services Authority
   B. International Accounting Standards Board
   C. International Accounting Standards Committee

3. U.S. Financial Accounting Standards are currently developed by which entity?
   A. U.S. Congress
   B. Financial Services Authority
   C. Financial Accounting Standards Board

4. The SEC requires which of the following be issued to shareholders before a shareholder meeting?
   A. Form 10-K
   B. Statement of cash flow
   C. Proxy statement

5. According to the *Framework for the Preparation and Presentation of Financial Statements*, which of the following is a qualitative characteristic of information in financial statements?
   A. Accuracy
   B. Timeliness
   C. Comparability

6. Which of the following is *not* a constraint on the financial statements according to the IFRS Framework?
   A. Timeliness
   B. Understandability
   C. Benefit versus cost

7. The assumption that an entity will continue to operate for the foreseeable future is called
   A. accrual basis.
   B. comparability.
   C. going concern.

8. The assumption that the effects of transactions and other events are recognized when they occur, not necessarily when cash movements occur, is called
   A. accrual basis.
   B. going concern.
   C. relevance.

9. Neutrality of information in the financial statements most closely contributes to which qualitative characteristic?
   A. Relevance
   B. Reliability
   C. Comparability

10. Does fair presentation entail full disclosure and transparency?

	Full Disclosure	**Transparency**
A.	No	Yes
B.	Yes	No
C.	Yes	Yes

11. Valuing assets at the amount of cash or equivalents paid, or the fair value of the consideration given to acquire them at the time of acquisition, most closely describes which measurement of financial statement elements?
    A. Current cost
    B. Realizable cost
    C. Historical cost

12. The valuation technique under which assets are recorded at the amount that would be received in an orderly disposal is
    A. current cost.
    B. present value.
    C. realizable value.

13. Which of the following is not a required financial statement according to IAS No. 1?
    A. Income statement
    B. Statement of changes in equity
    C. Statement of changes in income

14. Which of the following elements of financial statements is most closely related to measurement of performance?
    A. Assets
    B. Expenses
    C. Liabilities

15. Which of the following elements of financial statements is most closely related to measurement of financial position?
    A. Equity
    B. Income
    C. Expenses

16. Which of the following is not a characteristic of a coherent financial reporting framework?
    A. Timeliness
    B. Consistency
    C. Transparency

17. In the past, the Financial Accounting Standards Board has been criticized as having
    A. a rules-based approach to standards.
    B. a principles-based approach to standards.
    C. an objectives-oriented approach to standards.

18. Which of the following types of discussions regarding new accounting standards in management's discussion would provide the most meaningful information to an analyst?
    A. The standard does not apply.
    B. The impact of adoption is discussed.
    C. The standard will have no material impact.

CHAPTER 4

UNDERSTANDING THE INCOME STATEMENT

Thomas R. Robinson, CFA

CFA Institute
Charlottesville, Virginia

Hennie van Greuning, CFA

World Bank
Washington, DC

Elaine Henry, CFA

University of Miami
Miami, Florida

Michael A. Broihahn, CFA

Barry University
Miami, Florida

LEARNING OUTCOMES

After completing this chapter, you will be able to do the following:

- Describe the components of the income statement and the alternative presentation formats of that statement.
- Discuss the general principles of revenue recognition and accrual accounting, specific revenue recognition applications (including accounting for long-term contracts, installment

sales, barter transactions, gross and net reporting of revenue), and the implications of revenue recognition principles for financial analysis.
- Discuss the general principles of expense recognition, such as the matching principle, specific expense recognition applications (including depreciation of long-term assets and inventory methods), and the implications of expense recognition principles for financial analysis.
- Distinguish between the operating and nonoperating components of the income statement.
- Discuss the financial reporting treatment and analysis of nonrecurring items, including discontinued operations, extraordinary items, unusual or infrequent items, and changes in accounting standards.
- Describe the components of earnings per share and calculate a company's earnings per share (both basic and diluted earnings per share) for both a simple and complex capital structure.
- Evaluate a company's financial performance using common-size income statements and financial ratios based on the income statement.
- State the accounting classification for items that are excluded from the income statement but affect owners' equity, and list the major types of items receiving that treatment.
- Describe and calculate comprehensive income.

SUMMARY OVERVIEW

This chapter has presented the elements of income statement analysis. The income statement presents information on the financial results of a company's business activities over a period of time; it communicates how much revenue the company generated during a period and what costs it incurred in connection with generating that revenue. A company's net income and its components (e.g., gross margin, operating earnings, and pretax earnings) are critical inputs into both the equity and credit analysis processes. Equity analysts are interested in earnings because equity markets often reward relatively high- or low-earnings growth companies with above-average or below-average valuations, respectively. Fixed-income analysts examine the components of income statements, past and projected, for information on companies' abilities to make promised payments on their debt over the course of the business cycle. Corporate financial announcements frequently emphasize income statements more than the other financial statements. Key points to this chapter include the following:

- The income statement presents revenue, expenses, and net income.
- The components of the income statement include: revenue; cost of sales; sales, general, and administrative expenses; other operating expenses; nonoperating income and expenses; gains and losses; nonrecurring items; net income; and EPS.
- An income statement that presents a subtotal for gross profit (revenue minus cost of goods sold) is said to be presented in a multi-step format. One that does not present this subtotal is said to be presented in a single-step format.
- Revenue is recognized in the period it is earned, which may or may not be in the same period as the related cash collection. Recognition of revenue when earned is a fundamental principal of accrual accounting.
- In limited circumstances, specific revenue recognition methods may be applicable, including percentage of completion, completed contract, installment sales, and cost recovery.

- An analyst should identify differences in companies' revenue recognition methods and adjust reported revenue where possible to facilitate comparability. Where the available information does not permit adjustment, an analyst can characterize the revenue recognition as more or less conservative and thus qualitatively assess how differences in policies might affect financial ratios and judgments about profitability.

- The general principles of expense recognition include the matching principle. Expenses are matched either to revenue or to the time period in which the expenditure occurs (period costs) or to the time period of expected benefits of the expenditures (e.g. depreciation).

- In expense recognition, choice of method (i.e., depreciation method and inventory cost method), as well as estimates (i.e., uncollectible accounts, warranty expenses, assets' useful life, and salvage value) affect a company's reported income. An analyst should identify differences in companies' expense recognition methods and adjust reported financial statements where possible to facilitate comparability. Where the available information does not permit adjustment, an analyst can characterize the policies and estimates as more or less conservative and thus qualitatively assess how differences in policies might affect financial ratios and judgments about companies' performance.

- To assess a company's future earnings, it is helpful to separate those prior years' items of income and expense that are likely to continue in the future from those items that are less likely to continue.

- Some items from prior years clearly are not expected to continue in future periods and are separately disclosed on a company's income statement. Two such items are (1) discontinued operations and (2) extraordinary items. Both of these items are required to be reported separately from continuing operations.

- For other items on a company's income statement, such as unusual items and accounting changes, the likelihood of their continuing in the future is somewhat less clear and requires the analyst to make some judgments.

- Nonoperating items are reported separately from operating items. For example, if a non-financial service company invests in equity or debt securities issued by another company, any interest, dividends, or profits from sales of these securities will be shown as nonoperating income.

- Basic EPS is the amount of income available to common shareholders divided by the weighted average number of common shares outstanding over a period. The amount of income available to common shareholders is the amount of net income remaining after preferred dividends (if any) have been paid.

- If a company has a simple capital structure (i.e., one with no potentially dilutive securities), then its basic EPS is equal to its diluted EPS. If, however, a company has dilutive securities, its diluted EPS is lower than its basic EPS.

- Diluted EPS is calculated using the if-converted method for convertible securities and the treasury stock method for options.

- Common-size analysis of the income statement involves stating each line item on the income statement as a percentage of sales. Common-size statements facilitate comparison across time periods and across companies of different sizes.

- Two income-statement-based indicators of profitability are net profit margin and gross profit margin.

- Comprehensive income includes *both* net income and other revenue and expense items that are excluded from the net income calculation.

PROBLEMS

1. Expenses on the income statement may be grouped by
   A. nature, but not by function.
   B. function, but not by nature.
   C. either function or nature.

2. An example of an expense classification by function is
   A. tax expense.
   B. interest expense.
   C. cost of goods sold.

3. Denali Limited, a manufacturing company, had the following income statement information:

Revenue	$4,000,000
Cost of goods sold	$3,000,000
Other operating expenses	$500,000
Interest expense	$100,000
Tax expense	$120,000

   Denali's gross profit is equal to
   A. $280,000.
   B. $500,000.
   C. $1,000,000.

4. Under IFRS, income includes increases in economic benefits from
   A. increases in owners' equity related to owners' contributions.
   B. increases in liabilities not related to owners' contributions.
   C. enhancements of assets not related to owners' contributions.

5. Fairplay had the following information related to the sale of its products during 2006, which was its first year of business:

Revenue	$1,000,000
Returns of goods sold	$100,000
Cash collected	$800,000
Cost of goods sold	$700,000

   Under the accrual basis of accounting, how much net revenue would be reported on Fairplay's 2006 income statement?
   A. $200,000
   B. $800,000
   C. $900,000

6. If the outcome of a long-term contract can be measured reliably, the preferred accounting method under both IFRS and U.S. GAAP is

A. the installment method.
B. the completed contract method.
C. the percentage-of-completion method.

7. At the beginning of 2006, Florida Road Construction entered into a contract to build a road for the government. Construction will take four years. The following information as of 31 December 2006 is available for the contract:

Total revenue according to contract	$10,000,000
Total expected cost	$8,000,000
Cost incurred during 2006	$1,200,000

Under the completed contract method, how much revenue will be reported in 2006?
A. None
B. $300,000
C. $1,500,000

8. During 2006, Argo Company sold 10 acres of prime commercial zoned land to a builder for $5,000,000. The builder gave Argo a $1,000,000 down payment and will pay the remaining balance of $4,000,000 to Argo in 2007. Argo purchased the land in 1999 for $2,000,000. Using the installment method, how much profit will Argo report for 2006?
A. None
B. $600,000
C. $1,000,000

9. Using the same information as in Question 8, how much profit will Argo report for 2006 by using the cost recovery method?
A. None
B. $1,000,000
C. $3,000,000

10. Under IFRS, revenue from barter transactions should be measured based on the fair value of revenue from
A. similar barter transactions with related parties.
B. similar barter transactions with unrelated parties.
C. similar nonbarter transactions with unrelated parties.

11. Apex Consignment sells items over the Internet for individuals on a consignment basis. Apex receives the items from the owner, lists them for sale on the Internet, and receives a 25 percent commission for any items sold. Apex collects the full amount from the buyer and pays the net amount after commission to the owner. Unsold items are returned to the owner after 90 days. During 2006, Apex had the following information:

• Total sales price of items sold during 2006 on consignment was €2,000,000.
• Total commissions retained by Apex during 2006 for these items was €500,000.

How much revenue should Apex report on its 2006 income statement?
A. €500,000
B. €2,000,000
C. €1,500,000

12. During 2007, Accent Toys Plc., which began business in October of that year, purchased 10,000 units of its most popular toy at a cost of £10 per unit in October. In anticipation of heavy December sales, Accent purchased 5,000 additional units in November at a cost of £11 per unit. During 2007, Accent sold 12,000 units at a price of £15 per unit. Under the first in, first out (FIFO) method, what is Accent's cost of goods sold for 2007?
    A. £105,000
    B. £120,000
    C. £122,000

13. Using the same information as in Question 12, what would Accent's cost of goods sold be under the weighted average cost method?
    A. £120,000
    B. £122,000
    C. £124,000

14. Which inventory method is least likely to be used under IFRS?
    A. First in, first out (FIFO)
    B. Last in, first out (LIFO)
    C. Weighted average

15. At the beginning of 2007, Glass Manufacturing purchased a new machine for its assembly line at a cost of $600,000. The machine has an estimated useful life of 10 years and estimated residual value of $50,000. Under the straight-line method, how much depreciation would Glass take in 2008 for financial reporting purposes?
    A. None
    B. $55,000
    C. $60,000

16. Using the same information as in Question 15, how much depreciation would Glass take in 2007 for financial reporting purposes under the double-declining balance method?
    A. $60,000
    B. $110,000
    C. $120,000

17. Which combination of depreciation methods and useful lives is most conservative in the year a depreciable asset is acquired?
    A. Straight-line depreciation with a long useful life.
    B. Straight-line depreciation with a short useful life.
    C. Declining balance depreciation with a short useful life.

18. Under IFRS, a loss from the destruction of property in a fire would most likely be classified as
    A. continuing operations.
    B. an extraordinary item.
    C. discontinued operations.

19. For 2007, Flamingo Products had net income of $1,000,000. On 1 January 2007, there were 1,000,000 shares outstanding. On 1 July 2007, the company issued 100,000 new shares for $20 per share. The company paid $200,000 in dividends to common shareholders. What is Flamingo's basic earnings per share for 2007?
    A. $0.73
    B. $0.91
    C. $0.95

20. Cell Services (CSI) had 1,000,000 average shares outstanding during all of 2007. During 2007, CSI also had 10,000 options outstanding with exercise prices of $10 each. The average stock price of CSI during 2007 was $15. For purposes of computing diluted earnings per share, how many shares would be used in the denominator?
    A. 1,000,000
    B. 1,003,333
    C. 1,010,000

CHAPTER 5

UNDERSTANDING THE BALANCE SHEET

Thomas R. Robinson, CFA
CFA Institute
Charlottesville, Virginia

Hennie van Greuning, CFA
World Bank
Washington, DC

Elaine Henry, CFA
University of Miami
Miami, Florida

Michael A. Broihahn, CFA
Barry University
Miami, Florida

LEARNING OUTCOMES

After completing this chapter, you will be able to do the following:

- Define and interpret the asset and liability categories on the balance sheet, and discuss the uses of a balance sheet.
- Describe the various formats of balance sheet presentation.
- Compare and contrast current and noncurrent assets and liabilities.

- Explain the measurement bases (e.g., historical cost and fair value) of assets and liabilities, including current assets, current liabilities, tangible assets, and intangible assets.
- List and explain the appropriate classifications and related accounting treatments for financial instruments.
- List and explain the components of shareholders' equity.
- Interpret balance sheets, common-size balance sheets, the statement of changes in equity, and commonly used balance sheet ratios.

SUMMARY OVERVIEW

The starting place for analyzing a company is typically the balance sheet. It provides users such as creditors or investors with information regarding the sources of finance available for projects and infrastructure. At the same time, it normally provides information about the future earnings capacity of a company's assets as well as an indication of cash flows implicit in the receivables and inventories.

The balance sheet has many limitations, especially relating to the measurement of assets and liabilities. The lack of timely recognition of liabilities and, sometimes, assets, coupled with historical costs as opposed to fair value accounting for all items on the balance sheet, implies that the financial analyst must make numerous adjustments to determine the economic net worth of the company.

The balance sheet discloses what an entity owns (assets) and what it owes (liabilities) at a specific point in time, which is why it is also referred to as the statement of financial position. Equity represents the portion belonging to the owners or shareholders of a business. Equity is the residual interest in the assets of an entity after deducting its liabilities. The value of equity is increased by any generation of new assets by the business itself or by profits made during the year and is decreased by losses or withdrawals in the form of dividends.

The analyst must understand the structure and format of the balance sheet in order to evaluate the liquidity, solvency, and overall financial position of a company. Key points are:

- The "report format" of the balance sheet lists assets, liabilities, and equity in a single column. The "account format" follows the pattern of the traditional general ledger accounts, with assets at the left and liabilities and equity at the right of a central dividing line.
- The balance sheet should distinguish between current and noncurrent assets and between current and noncurrent liabilities unless a presentation based on liquidity provides more relevant and reliable information.
- Assets expected to be liquidated or used up within one year or one operating cycle of the business, whichever is greater, are classified as current assets. Assets not expected to be liquidated or used up within one year or one operating cycle of the business, whichever is greater, are classified as noncurrent assets.
- Liabilities expected to be settled or paid within one year or one operating cycle of the business, whichever is greater, are classified as current liabilities. Liabilities not expected to be settled or paid within one year or one operating cycle of the business, whichever is greater, are classified as noncurrent liabilities.
- Asset and liability values reported on a balance sheet may be measured on the basis of fair value or historical cost. Historical cost values may be quite different from economic values. Balance sheets must be evaluated critically in light of accounting policies applied in order to answer the question of how the values relate to economic reality and to each other.

- The notes to financial statements are an integral part of the U.S. GAAP and IFRS financial reporting processes. They provide important required detailed disclosures, as well as other information provided voluntarily by management. This information can be invaluable when determining whether the measurement of assets is comparable to other entities being analyzed.
- Tangible assets are long-term assets with physical substance that are used in company operations.
- Intangible assets are amounts paid by a company to acquire certain rights that are not represented by the possession of physical assets. A company should assess whether the useful life of an intangible asset is finite or infinite and, if finite, the length of its life.
- Under IFRS and U.S. GAAP, goodwill should be capitalized and tested for impairment annually. Goodwill is not amortized.
- Financial instruments are contracts that give rise to both a financial asset of one entity and a financial liability of another entity. Financial instruments come in a variety of instruments, including derivatives, hedges, and marketable securities.
- There are five potential components that comprise the owners' equity section of the balance: contributed capital, minority interest, retained earnings, treasury stock, and accumulated comprehensive income.
- The statement of changes in equity reflects information about the increases or decreases to a company's net assets or wealth.
- Ratio analysis is used by analysts and managers to assess company performance and status. Another valuable analytical technique is common-size (relative) analysis, which is achieved through the conversion of all balance sheet items to a percentage of total assets.

PROBLEMS

1. Resources controlled by a company as a result of past events are
   A. equity.
   B. assets.
   C. liabilities.

2. Equity equals
   A. Assets − Liabilities.
   B. Liabilities − Assets.
   C. Assets + Liabilities.

3. Distinguishing between current and noncurrent items on the balance sheet and presenting a subtotal for current assets and liabilities is referred to as
   A. the report format.
   B. the account format.
   C. a classified balance sheet.

4. All of the following are current assets *except*
   A. cash.
   B. goodwill.
   C. inventories.

5. Debt due within one year is considered
    A. current.
    B. preferred.
    C. long term.

6. Money received from customers for products to be delivered in the future is recorded as
    A. revenue and an asset.
    B. an asset and a liability.
    C. revenue and a liability.

7. The carrying value of inventories reflects
    A. their original cost.
    B. their current value.
    C. the lower of original cost or net realizable value.

8. When a company pays its rent in advance, its balance sheet will reflect a reduction in
    A. assets and liabilities.
    B. liabilities and shareholders' equity.
    C. one category of assets and an increase in another.

9. Accrued liabilities are
    A. balanced against an asset.
    B. expenses that have been paid.
    C. expenses that have been reported on the income statement.

10. The initial measurement of goodwill is
    A. not subject to management discretion.
    B. based on an acquisition's purchase price.
    C. based on the acquired company's book value.

11. Defining total asset turnover as revenue divided by average total assets, all else equal, impairment write-downs of long-lived assets owned by a company will most likely result in an increase for that company in
    A. the debt-to-equity ratio but not the total asset turnover.
    B. the total asset turnover but not the debt-to-equity ratio.
    C. both the debt-to-equity ratio and the total asset turnover.

12. For financial assets classified as trading securities, how are unrealized gains and losses reflected in shareholders' equity?
    A. They are not recognized.
    B. As an adjustment to paid-in capital.
    C. They flow through income into retained earnings.

13. For financial assets classified as available for sale, how are unrealized gains and losses reflected in shareholders' equity?
    A. They are not recognized.
    B. They flow through retained earnings.
    C. As a separate line item (other comprehensive income).

14. For financial assets classified as held to maturity, how are unrealized gains and losses reflected in shareholders' equity?
    A. They are not recognized.
    B. They flow through retained earnings.
    C. As a separate line item (valuation gains/losses).

15. Under IFRS, the minority interest in consolidated subsidiaries is presented on the balance sheet
    A. as a long-term liability.
    B. separately, but as a part of shareholders' equity.
    C. as a mezzanine item between liabilities and shareholders' equity.

16. Retained earnings are a component of
    A. liabilities.
    B. minority interest.
    C. owners' equity.

17. When a company buys shares of its own stock to be held in treasury, it records a reduction in
    A. both assets and liabilities.
    B. both assets and shareholders' equity.
    C. assets and an increase in shareholders' equity.

18. A common-size analysis of the balance sheet is most likely to signal investors that the company
    A. has increased sales.
    B. is using assets efficiently.
    C. is becoming more leveraged.

19. An investor concerned whether a company can meet its near-term obligations is most likely to calculate the
    A. current ratio.
    B. debt-to-equity ratio.
    C. return on total capital.

20. The most stringent test of a company's liquidity is its
    A. cash ratio.
    B. quick ratio.
    C. current ratio.

21. An investor worried that a company may go bankrupt would *most likely* examine its
    A. current ratio.
    B. return on equity.
    C. debt-to-equity ratio.

22. Using the information presented in Exhibit 5-8 in the chapter, the quick ratio for Sony Corp. on 31 March 2005 is *closest* to
    A. 0.44.
    B. 0.81.
    C. 0.84.

23. Applying common-size analysis to the Sony Corp. balance sheets presented in Exhibit 5-8, which one of the following line items increased in 2005 relative to 2004?
    A. Goodwill
    B. Securities investments and other
    C. Deferred insurance acquisition costs

24. Using the information presented in Exhibit 5-8, the financial leverage ratio for Sony Corp. on 31 March 2005 is *closest* to
    A. 2.30.
    B. 2.81.
    C. 3.31.

CHAPTER 6

UNDERSTANDING THE CASH FLOW STATEMENT

Thomas R. Robinson, CFA
CFA Institute
Charlottesville, Virginia

Hennie van Greuning, CFA
World Bank
Washington, DC

Elaine Henry, CFA
University of Miami
Miami, Florida

Michael A. Broihahn, CFA
Barry University
Miami, Florida

LEARNING OUTCOMES

After completing this chapter, you will be able to do the following:

- Compare and contrast cash flows from operating, investing, and financing activities and classify cash flow items as relating to one of those three categories given a description of the items.
- Describe how noncash investing and financing activities are reported.

33

- Compare and contrast the key differences in cash flow statements prepared under international financial reporting standards (IFRS) and U.S. generally accepted accounting principles (U.S. GAAP).
- Explain the difference between the direct and indirect method of presenting cash from operating activities and the arguments in favor of each method.
- Describe how the cash flow statement is linked to the income statement and the balance sheet.
- Explain the steps in the preparation of direct and indirect cash flow statements, including how cash flows can be computed using income statement and balance sheet data.
- Analyze and interpret a cash flow statement using both total currency amounts and common-size cash flow statements.
- Explain and compute free cash flow to the firm, free cash flow to equity, and other cash flow ratios.

SUMMARY OVERVIEW

The cash flow statement provides important information about a company's cash receipts and cash payments during an accounting period as well as information about a company's operating, investing, and financing activities. Although the income statement provides a measure of a company's success, cash and cash flow are also vital to a company's long-term success. Information on the sources and uses of cash helps creditors, investors, and other statement users evaluate the company's liquidity, solvency, and financial flexibility. Key concepts are as follows:

- Cash flow activities are classified into three categories: operating activities, investing activities, and financing activities. Significant noncash transaction activities (if present) are reported by using a supplemental disclosure note to the cash flow statement.
- The cash flow statement under IFRS is similar to U.S. GAAP; however, IFRS permits greater discretion in classifying some cash flow items as operating, investing, or financing activities.
- Companies can use either the direct or the indirect method for reporting their operating cash flow:
  ○ The direct method discloses operating cash inflows by source (e.g., cash received from customers, cash received from investment income) and operating cash outflows by use (e.g., cash paid to suppliers, cash paid for interest) in the operating activities section of the cash flow statement.
  ○ The indirect method reconciles net income to net cash flow from operating activities by adjusting net income for all noncash items and the net changes in the operating working capital accounts.
- The cash flow statement is linked to a company's income statement and comparative balance sheets and is constructed from the data on those statements.
- Although the indirect method is most commonly used by companies, the analyst can generally convert it to the direct format by following a simple three-step process.
- The analyst can use common-size statement analysis for the cash flow statement. Two prescribed approaches are the total cash inflows/total cash outflows method and the percentage of net revenues method.
- The cash flow statement can be used to determine FCFF and FCFE.
- The cash flow statement may also be used in financial ratios measuring a company's profitability, performance, and financial strength.

PROBLEMS

1. The three major classifications of activities in a cash flow statement are
   A. inflows, outflows, and balances.
   B. beginning balance, ending balance, and change.
   C. operating, investing, and financing.

2. The sale of a building for cash would be classified as what type of activity on the cash flow statement?
   A. Operating
   B. Investing
   C. Financing

3. Which of the following is an example of a financing activity on the cash flow statement under U.S. GAAP?
   A. Payment of dividends
   B. Receipt of dividends
   C. Payment of interest

4. A conversion of a face value $1 million convertible bond for $1 million of common stock would most likely be
   A. reported as a $1 million financing cash outflow and inflow.
   B. reported as supplementary information to the cash flow statement.
   C. reported as a $1 million financing cash outflow and a $1 million investing cash inflow.

5. Interest expense may be classified as an operating cash flow
   A. under U.S. GAAP, but may be classified as either operating or investing cash flows under IFRS.
   B. under IFRS, but may be classified as either operating or investing cash flows under U.S. GAAP.
   C. under U.S. GAAP, but may be classified as either operating or financing cash flows under IFRS.

6. Tax cash flows
   A. must be separately disclosed in the cash flow statement under IFRS only.
   B. must be separately disclosed in the cash flow statement under U.S. GAAP only.
   C. are not separately disclosed in the cash flow statement under IFRS or U.S. GAAP.

7. Which of the following components of the cash flow statement may be prepared under the indirect method under both IFRS and U.S. GAAP?
   A. Operating
   B. Investing
   C. Financing

8. Which of the following is most likely to appear in the operating section of a cash flow statement under the indirect method under U.S. GAAP?
   A. Net income
   B. Cash paid for interest
   C. Cash paid to suppliers

9. Red Road Company, a consulting company, reported total revenues of $100 million, total expenses of $80 million, and net income of $20 million in the most recent year. If accounts receivable increased by $10 million, how much cash did the company receive from customers?
   A. $110 million
   B. $90 million
   C. $30 million

10. Green Glory Corp., a garden supply wholesaler, reported cost of goods sold for the year of $80 million. Total assets increased by $55 million, including an increase of $5 million in inventory. Total liabilities increased by $45 million, including an increase of $2 million in accounts payable. How much cash did the company pay to its suppliers during the year?
    A. $90 million
    B. $83 million
    C. $77 million

11. Purple Fleur S.A., a retailer of floral products, reported cost of goods sold for the year of $75 million. Total assets increased by $55 million, but inventory declined by $6 million. Total liabilities increased by $45 million, and accounts payable increased by $2 million. How much cash did the company pay to its suppliers during the year?
    A. $85 million
    B. $79 million
    C. $67 million

12. White Flag, a women's clothing manufacturer, reported wage expense of $20 million. The beginning balance of wages payable was $3 million, and the ending balance of wages payable was $1 million. How much cash did the company pay in wages?
    A. $24 million
    B. $23 million
    C. $22 million

13. An analyst gathered the following information from a company's 2004 financial statements ($ millions):

Year Ended 31 December	2003	2004
Net sales	245.8	254.6
Cost of goods sold	168.3	175.9
Accounts receivable	73.2	68.3
Inventory	39.0	47.8
Accounts payable	20.3	22.9

Based only on the information above, the company's 2004 statement of cash flows prepared using the direct method would include amounts ($ millions) for cash received from customers and cash paid to suppliers, respectively, that are *closest* to:

	Cash Received from Customers	Cash Paid to Suppliers
A.	249.7	182.1
B.	259.5	169.7
C.	259.5	182.1

14. Golden Cumulus Corp., a commodities trading company, reported interest expense of
    $19 million and taxes of $6 million. Interest payable increased by $3 million, and taxes
    payable decreased by $4 million. How much cash did the company pay for interest and
    taxes?
    A. $22 million for interest and $2 million for taxes
    B. $16 million for interest and $2 million for taxes
    C. $16 million for interest and $10 million for taxes

15. An analyst gathered the following information from a company's 2005 financial statements
    ($ millions):

Balances as of Year Ended 31 December	2004	2005
Retained earnings	120	145
Accounts receivable	38	43
Inventory	45	48
Accounts payable	36	29

    The company declared and paid cash dividends of $10 million in 2005 and recorded
    depreciation expense in the amount of $25 million for 2005. The company's 2005 cash
    flow from operations ($ millions) was *closest* to
    A. 25.
    B. 35.
    C. 45.

16. Silverago Incorporated, an international metals company, reported a loss on the sale of
    equipment of $2 million. In addition, the company's income statement shows deprecia-
    tion expense of $8 million and the cash flow statement shows capital expenditure of $10
    million, all of which was for the purchase of new equipment. Using the following infor-
    mation from the comparative balance sheets, how much cash did the company receive
    from the equipment sale?

Balance Sheet Item	12/31/2005	12/31/2006	Change
Equipment	$100 million	$105 million	$5 million
Accumulated depreciation—equipment	$40 million	$46 million	$6 million

    A. $6 million
    B. $5 million
    C. $1 million

17. Jaderong Plinkett Stores reported net income of $25 million, which equals the compa-
    ny's comprehensive income. The company has no outstanding debt. Using the following
    information from the comparative balance sheets ($ millions), what should the company
    report in the financing section of the statement of cash flows?

Balance Sheet Item	12/31/2005	12/31/2006	Change
Common stock	$100	$102	$2
Additional paid-in capital common stock	$100	$140	$40
Retained earnings	$100	$115	$15
Total stockholders' equity	$300	$357	$57

A. Issuance of common stock $42 million; dividends paid of $10 million
B. Issuance of common stock $38 million; dividends paid of $10 million
C. Issuance of common stock $42 million; dividends paid of $40 million

18. Based on the following information for Pinkerly Inc., what are the total net adjustments that the company would make to net income in order to derive operating cash flow?

		Year Ended	
Income Statement Item		**12/31/2006**	
Net income		$20 million	
Depreciation		$2 million	
Balance Sheet Item	**12/31/2005**	**12/31/2006**	**Change**
Accounts receivable	$25 million	$22 million	($3 million)
Inventory	$10 million	$14 million	$4 million
Accounts payable	$8 million	$13 million	$5 million

A. Add $6 million
B. Add $8 million
C. Subtract $6 million

19. The first step in evaluating the cash flow statement should be to examine
A. individual investing cash flow items.
B. individual financing cash flow items.
C. the major sources and uses of cash.

20. Which of the following would be valid conclusions from an analysis of the cash flow statement for Telefónica Group presented in Exhibit 6-3 in the chapter?
A. The company does not pay dividends.
B. The primary use of cash is financing activities.
C. The primary source of cash is operating activities.

21. Which is an appropriate method of preparing a common-size cash flow statement?
A. Begin with net income and show the items that reconcile net income and operating cash flows.
B. Show each line item on the cash flow statement as a percentage of net revenue.
C. Show each line item on the cash flow statement as a percentage of total cash outflows.

22. Which of the following is an appropriate method of computing free cash flow to the firm?
A. Add operating cash flows plus capital expenditures and deduct after-tax interest payments.
B. Add operating cash flows plus after-tax interest payments and deduct capital expenditures.
C. Deduct both after-tax interest payments and capital expenditures from operating cash flows.

23. An analyst has calculated a ratio using as the numerator the sum of operating cash flow, interest, and taxes, and as the denominator the amount of interest. What is this ratio, what does it measure, and what does it indicate?

    A. This ratio is an interest coverage ratio, measuring a company's ability to meet its interest obligations and indicating a company's solvency.

    B. This ratio is an effective tax ratio, measuring the amount of a company's operating cash flow used for taxes, and indicating a company's efficiency in tax management.

    C. This ratio is an operating profitability ratio, measuring the operating cash flow generated accounting for taxes and interest, and indicating a company's liquidity.

FINANCIAL ANALYSIS TECHNIQUES

Thomas R. Robinson, CFA
CFA Institute
Charlottesville, Virginia

Hennie van Greuning, CFA
World Bank
Washington, DC

Elaine Henry, CFA
University of Miami
Miami, Florida

Michael A. Broihahn, CFA
Barry University
Miami, Florida

LEARNING OUTCOMES

After completing this chapter, you will be able to do the following:

- Identify the analytical phases, sources of information, and output of financial analysis.
- Differentiate between computation and analysis of ratios, and explain key questions that should be addressed in ratio analysis.

- Demonstrate and explain the use of ratio analysis, common-size financial statements, and graphs in company analysis and the value, purposes, and limitations of ratio analysis.
- Explain the common classifications of ratios and compute, analyze, and interpret activity, liquidity, solvency, profitability, and valuation ratios.
- Explain how ratios are related and how to evaluate a company using a combination of different ratios.
- Demonstrate the application of DuPont analysis (the decomposition of return on equity).
- Describe how ratios are useful in equity analysis.
- Describe how ratios are useful in credit analysis.
- Discuss segment reporting requirements and compute, analyze, and interpret segment ratios.
- Describe how the results of common-size and ratio analysis can be used to model/forecast earnings.

SUMMARY OVERVIEW

Financial analysis techniques, including common-size and ratio analysis, are useful in summarizing financial reporting data and evaluating the performance and financial position of a company. The results of financial analysis techniques provide important inputs into security valuation. Key facets of financial analysis include the following:

- Common-size financial statements and financial ratios remove the effect of size, allowing comparisons of a company with peer companies (cross-sectional analysis) and comparison of a company's results over time (trend or time-series analysis).
- Activity ratios measure the efficiency of a company's operations, such as collection of receivables or management of inventory. Major activity ratios include inventory turnover, days of inventory on hand, receivables turnover, days of sales outstanding, payables turnover, number of days of payables, working capital turnover, fixed asset turnover, and total asset turnover.
- Liquidity ratios measure the ability of a company to meet short-term obligations. Major liquidity ratios include the current ratio, quick ratio, cash ratio, and defensive interval ratio.
- Solvency ratios measure the ability of a company to meet long-term obligations. Major solvency ratios include debt ratios (including the debt-to-assets ratio, debt-to-capital ratio, debt-to-equity ratio, and financial leverage ratio) and coverage ratios (including interest coverage and fixed charge coverage).
- Profitability ratios measure the ability of a company to generate profits from revenue and assets. Major profitability ratios include return on sales ratios (including gross profit margin, operating profit margin, pretax margin, and net profit margin) and return on investment ratios (including operating ROA, ROA, ROE, and return on common equity).
- Ratios can also be combined and evaluated as a group to better understand how they fit together and how efficiency and leverage are tied to profitability.
- ROE can be analyzed as the product of the net profit margin, asset turnover, and financial leverage.
- Ratio analysis is useful in the selection and valuation of debt and equity securities and is a part of the credit rating process.
- Ratios can also be computed for business segments to evaluate how units within a business are doing.
- The results of financial analysis provide valuable inputs into forecasts of future earnings and cash flow.

PROBLEMS

1. Comparison of a company's financial results to other peer companies for the same time period is called
   A. horizontal analysis.
   B. time-series analysis.
   C. cross-sectional analysis.

2. In order to assess a company's ability to fulfill its long-term obligations, an analyst would *most likely* examine
   A. activity ratios.
   B. liquidity ratios.
   C. solvency ratios.

3. Which ratio would a company *most likely* use to measure its ability to meet short-term obligations?
   A. Current ratio
   B. Payables turnover
   C. Gross profit margin

4. Which of the following ratios would be *most useful* in determining a company's ability to cover its debt payments?
   A. ROA
   B. Total asset turnover
   C. Fixed charge coverage

5. John Chan is interested in assessing both the efficiency and liquidity of Spherion PLC. Chan has collected the following data for Spherion:

	2005	2004	2003
Days of inventory on hand	32	34	40
Days of sales outstanding	28	25	23
Number of days of payables	40	35	35

Based on this data, what is Chan *least likely* to conclude?
   A. Inventory management has contributed to improved liquidity.
   B. Management of payables has contributed to improved liquidity.
   C. Management of receivables has contributed to improved liquidity.

6. Marcus Lee is examining the solvency of Apex Manufacturing and has collected the following data (in millions of euros):

	2005	2004	2003
Total debt	€2,000	€1,900	€1,750
Total equity	€4,000	€4,500	€5,000

Which of the following would be the *most appropriate* conclusion for Lee?
A. The company is becoming increasingly less solvent, as evidenced by the increase in its debt-to-equity ratio from 0.35 to 0.50 from 2003 to 2005.
B. The company is becoming less liquid, as evidenced by the increase in its debt-to-equity ratio from 0.35 to 0.50 from 2003 to 2005.
C. The company is becoming increasingly more liquid, as evidenced by the increase in its debt-to-equity ratio from 0.35 to 0.50 from 2003 to 2005.

7. With regard to the data in Problem 6, what would be a reasonable explanation of these financial results?
A. The decline in the company's equity results from a decline in the market value of this company's common shares.
B. The increase of €250 in the company's debt from 2003 to 2005 indicates that lenders are viewing the company as increasingly creditworthy.
C. The decline in the company's equity indicates that the company may be incurring losses on its operations, paying dividends greater than income, and/or repurchasing shares.

8. Linda Roper observes a decrease in a company's inventory turnover. Which of the following would explain this trend?
A. The company installed a new inventory management system, allowing more efficient inventory management.
B. Due to problems with obsolescent inventory last year, the company wrote off a large amount of its inventory at the beginning of the period.
C. The company installed a new inventory management system but experienced some operational difficulties resulting in duplicate orders being placed with suppliers.

9. Which of the following would best explain an increase in receivables turnover?
A. The company adopted new credit policies last year and began offering credit to customers with weak credit histories.
B. Due to problems with an error in its old credit scoring system, the company had accumulated a substantial amount of uncollectible accounts and wrote off a large amount of its receivables.
C. To match the terms offered by its closest competitor, the company adopted new payment terms now requiring net payment within 30 days rather than 15 days, which had been its previous requirement.

10. Brown Corporation had an average days' sales outstanding of 19 days in 2005. Brown wants to decrease its collection period in 2006 to match the industry average of 15 days. Credit sales in 2005 were $300 million, and Brown expects credit sales to increase to $390 million in 2006. To achieve Brown's goal of decreasing the collection period, the change in the average accounts receivable balance from 2005 to 2006 that must occur is *closest* to
A. −$1.22 million.
B. −$0.42 million.
C. $0.42 million.

11. An analyst gathered the following data for a company:

	2003	2004	2005
ROE	19.8%	20.0%	22.0%
Return on total assets	8.1%	8.0%	7.9%
Total asset turnover	2.0	2.0	2.1

Based only on the information above, the *most* appropriate conclusion is that, over the period 2003 to 2005, the company's
A. net profit margin and financial leverage have decreased.
B. net profit margin and financial leverage have increased.
C. net profit margin has decreased but its financial leverage has increased.

12. A decomposition of ROE for Integra SA is as follows:

	2005	2004
ROE	18.90%	18.90%
Tax burden	0.70	0.75
Interest burden	0.90	0.90
EBIT margin	10.00%	10.00%
Asset turnover	1.50	1.40
Leverage	2.00	2.00

Which of the following choices *best* describes reasonable conclusions an analyst might make based on this ROE decomposition?
A. Profitability and the liquidity position both improved in 2005.
B. The higher average tax rate in 2005 offset the improvement in profitability, leaving ROE unchanged.
C. The higher average tax rate in 2005 offset the improvement in efficiency, leaving ROE unchanged.

13. A decomposition of ROE for Company A and Company B is as follows:

	Company A		Company B	
	2005	2004	2005	2004
ROE	26.46%	18.90%	26.33%	18.90%
Tax burden	0.7	0.75	0.75	0.75
Interest burden	0.9	0.9	0.9	0.9
EBIT margin	7.00%	10.00%	13.00%	10.00%
Asset turnover	1.5	1.4	1.5	1.4
Leverage	4	2	2	2

Which of the following choices *best* describes reasonable conclusions an analyst might make based on this ROE decomposition?

A. Company A's ROE is higher than Company B's in 2005, but the difference between the two companies' ROE is very small and was mainly the result of Company A's increase in its financial leverage.

B. Company A's ROE is higher than Company B's in 2005, apparently reflecting a strategic shift by Company A to a product mix with higher profit margins.

C. Company A's ROE is higher than Company B's in 2005, which suggests that Company A may have purchased new, more efficient equipment.

14. Rent-A-Center reported the following information related to total debt and shareholders' equity in its 2003 annual report.

| ($ thousands) | As of 31 December | | | | |
	2003	2002	2001	2000	1999
Total debt	698,000	521,330	702,506	741,051	847,160
Stockholders' equity	794,830	842,400	405,378	309,371	206,690

What would an analyst's most appropriate conclusion be based on this data?

A. The company's solvency improved from 1999 to 2002.

B. The company's solvency improved from 2002 to 2003.

C. The data suggest the company increased debt in 2002.

15. Frank Collins observes the following data for two companies:

	Company A	Company B
Revenue	$4,500	$6,000
Net income	$50	$1,000
Current assets	$40,000	$60,000
Total assets	$100,000	$700,000
Current liabilities	$10,000	$50,000
Total debt	$60,000	$150,000
Shareholders' equity	$30,000	$500,000

Which of the following choices best describes reasonable conclusions that Collins might make about the two companies' ability to pay their current and long-term obligations?

A. Company A's current ratio of 4.0x indicates it is more liquid than Company B, whose current ratio is only 1.2x, but Company B is more solvent, as indicated by its lower debt-to-equity ratio.

B. Company A's current ratio of 25 percent indicates it is less liquid than Company B, whose current ratio is 83 percent, and Company A is also less solvent, as indicated by a debt-to-equity ratio of 200 percent compared with Company B's debt-to-equity ratio of only 30 percent.

C. Company A's current ratio of 4.0x indicates it is more liquid than Company B, whose current ratio is only 1.2x, and Company A is also more solvent, as indicated by a debt-to-equity ratio of 200 percent compared with Company B's debt-to-equity ratio of only 30 percent.

Use the following information to answer Problems 16 through 19.

The data below appear in the five-year summary of a major international company. A business combination with another major manufacturer took place in 2003. The term *turnover* in this financial data is a synonym for revenue.

	2000	2001	2002	2003	2004
Financial statements	GBP m	GBP m	GBP m	GBP m	GBP m
Income statements					
Turnover (i.e., revenue)	4,390	3,624	3,717	8,167	11,366
Profit before interest and taxation (EBIT)	844	700	704	933	1,579
Net interest payable	−80	−54	−98	−163	−188
Taxation	−186	−195	−208	−349	−579
Minorities	−94	−99	−105	−125	−167
Profit for the year	484	352	293	296	645
Balance sheets					
Fixed assets	3,510	3,667	4,758	10,431	11,483
Current asset investments, cash at bank and in hand	316	218	290	561	682
Other current assets	558	514	643	1,258	1,634
Total assets	4,384	4,399	5,691	12,250	13,799
Interest bearing debt (long term)	−602	−1,053	−1,535	−3,523	−3,707
Other creditors and provisions (current)	−1,223	−1,054	−1,102	−2,377	−3,108
Total liabilities	−1,825	−2,107	−2,637	−5,900	−6,815
Net assets	2,559	2,292	3,054	6,350	6,984
Shareholders' funds	2,161	2,006	2,309	5,572	6,165
Equity minority interests	398	286	745	778	819
Capital employed	2,559	2,292	3,054	6,350	6,984
Cash flow					
Working capital movements	−53	5	71	85	107
Net cash inflow from operating activities	864	859	975	1,568	2,292

16. The company's total assets at year-end 1999 were GBP 3,500 million. Which of the following choices *best* describes reasonable conclusions an analyst might make about the company's efficiency?
    A. Comparing 2004 with 2000, the company's efficiency improved, as indicated by a total asset turnover ratio of 0.86 compared with 0.64.
    B. Comparing 2004 with 2000, the company's efficiency deteriorated, as indicated by its current ratio.
    C. Comparing 2004 with 2000, the company's efficiency deteriorated due to asset growth faster than turnover (i.e., revenue) growth.

17. Which of the following choices *best* describes reasonable conclusions an analyst might make about the company's solvency?
    A. Comparing 2004 with 2000, the company's solvency improved, as indicated by an increase in its debt-to-assets ratio from 0.14 to 0.27.
    B. Comparing 2004 with 2000, the company's solvency deteriorated, as indicated by a decrease in interest coverage from 10.6 to 8.4.
    C. Comparing 2004 with 2000, the company's solvency improved, as indicated by the growth in its profits to GBP 645 million.

18. Which of the following choices *best* describes reasonable conclusions an analyst might make about the company's liquidity?
    A. Comparing 2004 with 2000, the company's liquidity improved, as indicated by an increase in its debt-to-assets ratio from 0.14 to 0.27.
    B. Comparing 2004 with 2000, the company's liquidity deteriorated, as indicated by a decrease in interest coverage from 10.6 to 8.4.
    C. Comparing 2004 with 2000, the company's liquidity improved, as indicated by an increase in its current ratio from 0.71 to 0.75.

19. Which of the following choices *best* describes reasonable conclusions an analyst might make about the company's profitability?
    A. Comparing 2004 with 2000, the company's profitability improved, as indicated by an increase in its debt-to-assets ratio from 0.14 to 0.27.
    B. Comparing 2004 with 2000, the company's profitability deteriorated, as indicated by a decrease in its net profit margin from 11.0 percent to 5.7 percent.
    C. Comparing 2004 with 2000, the company's profitability improved, as indicated by the growth in its shareholders' equity to GBP 6,165 million.

20. In general, a creditor would consider a decrease in which of the following ratios to be positive news?
    A. Interest coverage (times interest earned)
    B. Debt to total assets
    C. Return on assets

21. Assuming no changes in other variables, which of the following would decrease ROA?
    A. A decrease in the effective tax rate
    B. A decrease in interest expense
    C. An increase in average assets

22. What does the P/E ratio measure?
    A. The "multiple" that the stock market places on a company's EPS.
    B. The relationship between dividends and market prices.
    C. The earnings for one common share of stock.

CHAPTER 8

INTERNATIONAL STANDARDS CONVERGENCE

Thomas R. Robinson, CFA
CFA Institute
Charlottesville, Virginia

Hennie van Greuning, CFA
World Bank
Washington, DC

Elaine Henry, CFA
University of Miami
Miami, Florida

Michael A. Broihahn, CFA
Barry University
Miami, Florida

LEARNING OUTCOMES

After completing this chapter, you will be able to do the following:

- State and explain key aspects of the International Financial Reporting Standards (IFRS) framework as they pertain to the objectives and qualitative characteristics of financial statements.

- Identify and explain the major international accounting standards for each asset and liability category on the balance sheet, and the key differences from U.S. generally accepted accounting principles (GAAP).
- Identify and explain the major international accounting standards for major revenue and expense categories on the income statement, and the key differences from U.S. GAAP.
- Identify and explain the major differences between international and U.S. GAAP accounting standards concerning the treatment of interest and dividends on the cash flow statement.
- Interpret the effect of differences between international and U.S. GAAP accounting standards on the balance sheet, income statement, and the statement of changes in equity for some commonly used financial ratios.

SUMMARY OVERVIEW

The IASB is the standard-setting body of the IASC Foundation. The objectives of the IASC Foundation are to develop a single set of global financial reporting standards and to promote the use of those standards. In accomplishing these objectives, the IASC Foundation explicitly aims to bring about convergence between national standards and international standards. Many national accounting standard setters have adopted, or are in the process of adopting, the IFRS.

This chapter discussed both the IFRS Framework and the IFRS standards for reporting accounting items on the balance sheet, income statement, and cash flow statement. Key points include the following:

- The objectives of financial statements, as stated in the Framework, are "to provide information about the financial position, performance, and changes in financial position of an entity; this information should be useful to a wide range of users for the purpose of making economic decisions."
- To achieve the objective of providing useful information, financial statements should have the following qualitative characteristics: relevance, predictive value, faithful representation, neutrality, and verifiability.
- Financial statements provide information on the financial position and performance of an entity by grouping the effects of transactions and other events into the following five broad elements: assets, liabilities, equity, income, and expenses.
- Both IFRS and U.S. GAAP require companies to present basic financial statements: balance sheet, income statement, statement of cash flows, and statement of changes in equity.
- One major difference between IFRS and U.S. GAAP affecting all three statements involves inventories: U.S. GAAP allows the LIFO method for inventory costing, whereas IFRS does not.
- Another major balance sheet difference between IFRS and U.S. GAAP is that IFRS allows companies to revalue property, plant, and equipment as well as intangible assets.
- Accounting for investments is another area of difference: IFRS uses a voting control model to determine need for consolidation, whereas U.S. GAAP uses a dual model based on voting control and economic control.
- An important difference between IFRS and U.S. GAAP is the treatment of some nonrecurring items. IFRS does not permit any items to be classified as extraordinary items.
- International standards allow companies to report cash inflows from interest and dividends as relating to either operating or investing activities, and cash outflows for interest and dividends as relating to either operating or financing activities.

- Convergence between IFRS and U.S. GAAP has increased significantly over the past few years and is continuing.
- Analysts should know how to make financial statement adjustments to better compare IFRS reporting companies with those companies reporting under U.S. GAAP.

PROBLEMS

1. According to the IFRS Framework, which of the following is a qualitative characteristic related to the usefulness of information in financial statements?
   A. Neutrality
   B. Timeliness
   C. Accrual basis

2. Under the IFRS Framework, changes in the elements of financial statements are *most likely* portrayed in the
   A. balance sheet.
   B. income statement.
   C. cash flow statement.

3. Under IASB standards, which of the following categories of marketable securities is *most likely* to incur an asymmetrical treatment of income and changes in value?
   A. Held for trading
   B. Held to maturity
   C. Available for sale

4. According to IASB standards, which of the following inventory methods is *most preferred?*
   A. Specific identification
   B. Weighted average cost
   C. First in, first out (FIFO)

5. According to IASB standards, which of the following inventory methods is not acceptable?
   A. Weighted average cost
   B. First in, first out (FIFO)
   C. Last in, first out (LIFO)

6. Under IASB standards, inventory write-downs are
   A. not allowed.
   B. allowed but not reversible.
   C. allowed and subject to reversal.

7. According to IASB standards, property, plant, and equipment revaluations are
   A. not allowed.
   B. allowed for decreases only.
   C. allowed for both increases and decreases.

8. Under IASB standards, a joint venture interest is accounted for by using
   A. consolidation.
   B. the equity method or consolidation.
   C. the equity method or proportionate consolidation.

9. Under IASB standards, goodwill
   A. may be written off when acquired.
   B. is subject to an annual impairment test.
   C. is amortized over its expected useful life.

10. Under IASB standards, negative goodwill
    A. must be recorded as a gain.
    B. is prorated to the noncurrent assets.
    C. is accounted for as an extraordinary item.

11. Under IASB standards, an identifiable intangible asset with an indefinite life
    A. may be written off when acquired.
    B. is amortized over a 20-year period.
    C. is accounted for in the same manner as goodwill.

12. Under IASB standards, identifiable intangible assets are
    A. only revalued downward, with the decrease reported to profit and loss.
    B. revalued upward and reported to equity when reversing a previous revaluation decrease.
    C. revalued upward and reported to profit and loss when reversing a previous revaluation decrease.

13. Under IASB standards, when the outcome of a construction contract cannot be estimated reliably, revenue and costs should be
    A. recognized by using the completed contract method.
    B. recognized by using the percentage of completion contract method.
    C. recognized to the extent that it is probable to recover contract costs.

14. Under IASB standards, fixed asset depreciation methods must be
    A. rational and systematic.
    B. rational and reviewed at least annually.
    C. systematic and reflect the pattern of expected consumption.

15. Under IASB standards, cash inflows for the receipt of interest and dividends are
    A. operating cash flows.
    B. either operating or investing cash flows.
    C. either investing or financing cash flows.

16. Under IASB standards, cash outflows for the payment of interest are
    A. operating cash flows.
    B. either investing or financing cash flows.
    C. either operating or financing cash flows.

17. Under IASB standards, cash outflows for the payment of dividends are
    A. financing cash flows.
    B. either operating or investing cash flows.
    C. either operating or financing cash flows.

18. When comparing a U.S. company that uses LIFO accounting with an IFRS company that uses FIFO accounting, an analyst will
    A. make no adjustment if the adjustment data are unavailable.
    B. adjust either company to achieve comparability with the other.
    C. adjust the U.S. company to achieve comparability with the IFRS company.

19. When comparing a U.S. company with an IFRS company that has written up the value of its intangible assets, an analyst will eliminate the effect of the write-ups in calculating the
    A. gross margin.
    B. earnings per share.
    C. financial leverage multiplier.

FINANCIAL STATEMENT ANALYSIS: APPLICATIONS

Thomas R. Robinson, CFA

CFA Institute
Charlottesville, Virginia

Hennie van Greuning, CFA

World Bank
Washington, DC

Elaine Henry, CFA

University of Miami
Miami, Florida

Michael A. Broihahn, CFA

Barry University
Miami, Florida

LEARNING OUTCOMES

After completing this chapter, you will be able to do the following:

- Evaluate a company's past financial performance and explain how a company's strategy is reflected in past financial performance.
- Prepare a basic projection of a company's future net income and cash flow.

- Describe the role of financial statement analysis in assessing the credit quality of a potential debt investment.
- Discuss the use of financial statement analysis in screening for potential equity investments.
- Determine and justify appropriate analyst adjustments to a company's financial statements to facilitate comparison with another company.

SUMMARY OVERVIEW

This chapter describes selected applications of financial statement analysis, including the evaluation of past financial performance, the projection of future financial performance, the assessment of credit risk, and the screening of potential equity investments. In addition, the chapter introduced analyst adjustments to reported financials. In all cases, the analyst needs to have a good understanding of the financial reporting standards under which financial statements are prepared. Because standards evolve over time, analysts must stay current in order to make good investment decisions. The main points in the chapter include the following:

- Evaluating a company's historical performance addresses not only what happened but also the causes behind the company's performance and how the performance reflects the company's strategy.
- The projection of a company's future net income and cash flow often begins with a top-down sales forecast in which the analyst forecasts industry sales and the company's market share. By projecting profit margins or expenses and the level of investment in working and fixed capital needed to support projected sales, the analyst can forecast net income and cash flow.
- Projections of future performance are needed for discounted cash flow valuation of equity and are often needed in credit analysis to assess a borrower's ability to repay interest and principal of a debt obligation.
- Credit analysis uses financial statement analysis to evaluate credit-relevant factors, including tolerance for leverage, operational stability, and margin stability.
- When ratios using financial statement data and market data are used to screen for potential equity investments, fundamental decisions include which metrics to use as screens, how many metrics to include, what values of those metrics to use as cutoff points, and what weighting to give each metric.
- Analyst adjustments to a company's reported financial statements are sometimes necessary (e.g., when comparing companies that use different accounting methods or assumptions). Adjustments include those related to investments; inventory; property, plant, and equipment; goodwill; and off-balance-sheet financing.

PROBLEMS

1. Projecting profit margins into the future on the basis of past results would be *most* reliable when the company
   A. is a large, diversified company operating in mature industries.
   B. is in the commodities business.
   C. operates in a single business segment.

2. Galambos Corporation had an average receivable collection period of 19 days in 2003. Galambos has stated that it wants to decrease its collection period in 2004 to match the industry average of 15 days. Credit sales in 2003 were $300 million, and analysts expect credit sales to increase to $400 million in 2004. To achieve the company's goal of decreasing the collection period, the change in the average accounts receivable balance from 2003 to 2004 that must occur is *closest* to
   A. –$420,000.
   B. $420,000.
   C. $836,000.

3. Credit analysts are likely to consider which of the following in making a rating recommendation?
   A. Business risk, but not financial risk
   B. Financial risk, but not business risk
   C. Both business risk and financial risk

4. When screening for potential equity investments based on return on equity, to control risk an analyst would be *most likely* to include a criterion that requires
   A. positive net income.
   B. negative net income.
   C. negative shareholders' equity.

5. One concern when screening for low price-to-earnings stocks is that companies with low price-to-earnings ratios may be financially weak. What criteria might an analyst include to avoid inadvertently selecting weak companies?
   A. current-year sales growth lower than prior-year sales growth
   B. net income less than zero
   C. debt-to-total assets ratio below a certain cutoff point

6. When a database eliminates companies that cease to exist because of a merger or bankruptcy, this can result in
   A. look-ahead bias.
   B. backtesting bias.
   C. survivorship bias.

7. In a comprehensive financial analysis, financial statements should be
   A. used as reported without adjustment.
   B. adjusted after completing ratio analysis.
   C. adjusted for differences in accounting standards, such as IFRS and U.S. GAAP.

8. When comparing financial statements prepared under IFRS with those prepared under U.S. GAAP, analysts may need to make adjustments related to
   A. realized losses.
   B. unrealized gains and losses for trading securities.
   C. unrealized gains and losses for available-for-sale securities.

9. When comparing a U.S. company using the LIFO method of inventory to companies preparing their financial statements under IFRS, analysts should be aware that according to IFRS, the LIFO method of inventory

A. is never acceptable.
B. is always acceptable.
C. is acceptable when applied to finished goods inventory only.

10. An analyst is evaluating the balance sheet of a U.S. company that uses LIFO accounting for inventory. The analyst collects the following data:

	31 Dec 05	31 Dec 06
Inventory reported on balance sheet	$500,000	$600,000
LIFO reserve	$50,000	$70,000
Average tax rate	30%	30%

After adjustment to convert to FIFO, inventory on 31 December 2006 would be closest to
A. $600,000.
B. $620,000.
C. $670,000.

11. An analyst gathered the following data for a company ($ millions):

	31 Dec 2000	31 Dec 2001
Gross investment in fixed assets	$2.8	$2.8
Accumulated depreciation	$1.2	$1.6

The average age and average depreciable life, respectively, of the company's fixed assets at the end of 2001 are *closest* to

	Average Age	Average Depreciable Life
A.	1.75 years	7 years
B.	1.75 years	14 years
C.	4.00 years	7 years

12. To compute tangible book value, an analyst would
A. add goodwill to stockholders' equity.
B. add all intangible assets to stockholders' equity.
C. subtract all intangible assets from stockholders' equity.

13. Which of the following is an off-balance-sheet financing technique? The use of
A. the LIFO inventory method.
B. capital leases.
C. operating leases.

14. To better evaluate the solvency of a company, an analyst would most likely add to total liabilities
A. the present value of future capital lease payments.
B. the total amount of future operating lease payments.
C. the present value of future operating lease payments.

CHAPTER 10

INVENTORIES

Elbie Antonites, CFA
University of Pretoria
Pretoria, South Africa

Michael A. Broihahn, CFA
Barry University
Miami, Florida

LEARNING OUTCOMES

After completing this chapter, you will be able to do the following:

- Explain International Financial Reporting Standards (IFRS) and U.S. generally accepted accounting principles (U.S. GAAP) rules for determining inventory cost including which costs are capitalized and methods of allocating costs between cost of goods sold and inventory.
- Discuss how inventories are reported in the financial statements and how the lower of cost or net realizable value is used and applied.
- Compute ending inventory balances and cost of goods sold using the first in, first out (FIFO), weighted average cost, and last in, first out (LIFO) methods to account for product inventory and explain the relationship among and the usefulness of inventory and cost of goods sold data provided by the FIFO, weighted average cost, and LIFO methods when prices are (1) stable, (2) decreasing, or (3) increasing.
- Discuss ratios useful for evaluating inventory management.
- Analyze the financial statements of companies using different inventory accounting methods to compare and describe the effect of the different methods on cost of goods sold, inventory balances, and other financial statement items; and compute and describe the effects of the choice of inventory method on profitability, liquidity, activity, and solvency ratios.
- Make adjustments to reported financial statements related to inventory assumptions in order to aid in comparing and evaluating companies.

• Discuss the reasons that a LIFO reserve might rise or decline during a given period and discuss the implications for financial analysis.

SUMMARY OVERVIEW

Inventory cost flow is a major determinant in measuring income for merchandising and manufacturing companies. In addition, inventories are usually a significant asset on the balance sheets of these companies. The financial statements and financial notes of a company provide important information that the analyst needs to correctly assess and compare financial performance with other companies. Key concepts in this chapter are as follows:

• Inventories are a major factor in the analysis of merchandising and manufacturing companies. Such companies generate their sales and profits through inventory transactions on a regular basis. An important consideration in determining profits for these companies is measuring the cost of goods sold when inventories are sold to business customers.
• The cost of inventories comprises all costs of purchase, costs of conversion, and other costs incurred in bringing the inventories to their present location and condition. Also, any allocation of fixed production overhead is based on normal capacity levels, with unallocated production overhead expensed as incurred.
• Under IFRS, the cost of inventories is assigned by using either the FIFO or weighted average cost formula. The specific identification method is required for inventories of items that are not ordinarily interchangeable and for goods or services produced and segregated for specific projects. A business entity must use the same cost formula for all inventories having a similar nature and use to the entity.
• Inventories are measured at the lower of cost or "net realizable value." Net realizable value is the estimated selling price in the ordinary course of business less the estimated costs necessary to make the sale. Reversals of write-downs are permissible under IFRS but not U.S. GAAP.
• The choice of inventory method impacts the financial statements and any financial ratios that are derived from them. As a consequence, the analyst must carefully consider inventory method differences when evaluating a company's performance or when comparing a company with industry data or industry competitors.
• The inventory turnover ratio, number of days of inventory ratio, and gross profit margin ratio are directly and fully affected by a company's choice of inventory method.
• Under U.S. GAAP, the LIFO method is widely used for both tax and financial reporting purposes because of potential income tax savings.
• LIFO reserve liquidation occurs when the number of units in ending inventory declines from the number of units that were present at the beginning of the year. If inventory unit costs have generally risen from year to year, the phenomenon of inventory "phantom" gross profits occurs on liquidation.
• Under U.S. GAAP, companies that use the LIFO inventory method must disclose in their financial notes the amount of the LIFO reserve or the amount that would have been reported in inventory if the FIFO method had been used.
• Consistency of inventory costing is required under both U.S. GAAP and IFRS. If a company changes an accounting policy, the change must be justifiable and all financial statements are accounted for retrospectively.

PROBLEMS

1. Inventory cost is *least likely* to include
    A. production-related storage costs.
    B. costs incurred due to normal waste of materials.
    C. transportation costs of shipping inventory to customers.

2. Ajax Factories produces pencils at a factory designed to produce 10 million pencils per year. In 2007 the fixed production overhead related to the factory was $1 million and the factory produced 9 million pencils. The inventory cost for each pencil related to the fixed production overhead is *closest* to
    A. $0.00
    B. $0.10
    C. $0.11

3. Mustard Seed PLC adheres to IFRS. It recently purchased inventory for €100 million and spent €5 million for storage prior to selling the goods. The amount it charged to inventory expense (in € millions) was *closest* to
    A. €95.
    B. €100.
    C. €105.

4. Carrying inventory at a value above its historical cost would *most likely* be permitted if
    A. the inventory was held by a produce dealer.
    B. financial statements were prepared using U.S. GAAP.
    C. the change resulted from a reversal of a previous write-down.

5. Eric's Used Bookstore prepares its financial statements in accordance with U.S. GAAP. Inventory was purchased for $1 million and later marked down to $550,000. However, one of the books was later discovered to be a rare collectible item and the inventory is now worth an estimated $3 million. The inventory is *most likely* reported on the balance sheet at
    A. $550,000.
    B. $1,000,000.
    C. $3,000,000.

6. Fernando's Pasta purchased inventory and later wrote it down, though the current realizable value is higher than the value when written down. Fernando's inventory balance will *most likely* be
    A. higher if it complies with IFRS.
    B. higher if it complies with U.S. GAAP.
    C. the same under U.S. GAAP and IFRS.

7. Cinnamon Corp. started business in 2007 and uses the weighted average cost inventory method. During 2007 it purchased 45,000 units of inventory at €10 each and sold 40,000 units for €20 each. In 2008 it purchased another 50,000 units at €11 each

and sold 45,000 units for €22 each. Its 2008 cost of goods sold (in € thousands) was *closest* to
   A. €490.
   B. €491.
   C. €495.

8. Zimt AG started business in 2007 and uses the FIFO inventory method. During 2007 it purchased 45,000 units of inventory at €10 each and sold 40,000 units for €20 each. In 2008 it purchased another 50,000 units at €11 each and sold 45,000 units for €22 each. Its 2008 ending inventory balance (in € thousands) was *closest* to
   A. €105.
   B. €109.
   C. €110.

9. Zimt AG uses the FIFO inventory accounting method, and Nutmeg Inc. uses the LIFO method. Compared to the cost of replacing the inventory, during periods of rising prices the cost of goods sold reported by
   A. Zimt is too low.
   B. Nutmeg is too low.
   C. Nutmeg is too high.

10. Zimt AG uses the FIFO inventory accounting method, and Nutmeg Inc. uses the LIFO method. Compared to the cost of replacing the inventory, during periods of rising prices the ending inventory balance reported by
    A. Zimt is too high.
    B. Nutmeg is too low.
    C. Nutmeg is too high.

11. Like many technology companies, TechnoTools operates in an environment of declining prices. Its reported profits will tend to be *highest* if it accounts for inventory using the
    A. FIFO method.
    B. LIFO method.
    C. weighted average cost method.

12. Compared to using the weighted average cost method to account for inventory, during a period in which prices are generally rising the current ratio of a company using the FIFO method would *most likely* be
    A. lower.
    B. higher.
    C. dependent upon the interaction with accounts payable.

13. Zimt AG wrote down the value of inventory in 2007 and reversed the write-down in 2008. Compared to ratios calculated if the write-down had never occurred, Zimt's reported 2007
    A. current ratio was too high.
    B. gross margin was too high.
    C. inventory turnover was too high.

14. Zimt AG wrote down the value of inventory in 2007 and reversed the write-down in 2008. Compared to results reported if the write-down had never occurred, Zimt's reported 2008
    A. profit was overstated.
    B. cash flow from operations was overstated.
    C. year-end inventory balance was overstated.

15. Compared to a company that uses the FIFO inventory accounting method, during periods of rising prices a company that uses the LIFO method will *most likely* appear more
    A. liquid.
    B. efficient.
    C. profitable.

16. Nutmeg, Inc. uses the LIFO method to account for inventory. During years in which inventory unit costs are generally rising and in which the company purchases more inventory than it sells to customers its reported gross profit margin will *most likely* be
    A. lower than it would have been if the company used the FIFO method.
    B. higher than it would have been if the company used the FIFO method.
    C. about the same as it would have been if the company used the FIFO method.

17. Sauerbraten Corp. reported 2007 sales ($ in millions) of $2,157 and cost of goods sold of $1,827. The company uses the LIFO method for inventory valuation and discloses that if the FIFO inventory valuation method had been used, inventories would have been $63.3 million and $56.8 million higher in 2007 and 2006, respectively. If Sauerbraten used the FIFO method exclusively, it would have reported 2007 gross profit *closest* to
    A. $324.
    B. $330.
    C. $337.

18. Sauerbraten Corp. reported 2007 sales ($ in millions) of $2,157 and cost of goods sold of $1,827. Inventories at year-end 2007 and 2006, respectively, were $553 and $562. The company uses the LIFO method for inventory valuation and discloses that if the FIFO inventory valuation method had been used, inventories would have been $63.3 million and $56.8 million higher in 2007 and 2006, respectively. Compared to the inventory turnover ratio reported, if Sauerbraten had exclusively used the FIFO method its inventory turnover ratio would have been *closest* to
    A. 2.96.
    B. 3.28.
    C. 3.49.

19. Compared to using the FIFO method to account for inventory, during periods of rising prices a company that uses the LIFO method is *most likely* to report higher
    A. net income.
    B. cost of sales.
    C. income taxes.

20. In order to compare the results of a company that uses the LIFO method to one using
    FIFO, the required adjustments to the financial statements of the LIFO user include
    adding the
    A. LIFO reserve to inventory.
    B. change in the LIFO reserve to inventory.
    C. change in the LIFO reserve to cost of goods sold.

21. Carey Company adheres to U.S. GAAP, while Jonathan Company adheres to IFRS. It is
    least likely that
    A. Carey has reversed an inventory write-down.
    B. Jonathan has reversed an inventory write-down.
    C. Jonathan and Carey both use the FIFO inventory accounting method.

CHAPTER 11

LONG-LIVED ASSETS

Elaine Henry, CFA
University of Miami
Coral Gables, Florida

Elizabeth A. Gordon
Temple University
Philadelphia, Pennsylvania

LEARNING OUTCOMES

After completing this chapter, you will be able to do the following:

- Explain the accounting standards related to the capitalization of expenditures as part of long-lived assets, including interest costs.
- Compute and describe the effects of capitalizing versus expensing on net income, shareholders' equity, cash flow from operations, and financial ratios including the effect on the interest coverage ratio of capitalizing interest costs.
- Explain the circumstances in which software development costs and research and development costs are capitalized.
- Identify the different depreciation methods for long-lived tangible assets and discuss how the choice of method, useful lives, and salvage values affect a company's financial statements, ratios, and taxes.
- Discuss the use of fixed asset disclosures to compare companies' average age of depreciable assets, and calculate, using such disclosures, the average age and average depreciable life of fixed assets.
- Describe amortization of intangible assets with finite useful lives, and the estimates that affect the amortization calculations.
- Discuss the liability for closure, removal, and environmental effects of long-lived operating assets, and discuss the financial statement impact and ratio effects of that liability.
- Discuss the impact of sales or exchanges of long-lived assets on financial statements.

- Define impairment of long-lived tangible and intangible assets and explain what effect such impairment has on a company's financial statements and ratios.
- Calculate and describe both the initial and long-lived effects of asset revaluations on financial ratios.

SUMMARY OVERVIEW

Key points include the following:

- Expenditures related to long-lived assets are included as part of the value of assets on the balance sheet (i.e., capitalized) if they are expected to provide future benefits, typically beyond one year.
- Although capitalizing expenditures, rather than expensing, results in higher reported profitability in the initial year, it results in lower profitability in subsequent years; however, if a company continues to purchase similar or increasing amounts of assets each year, the profitability-enhancing effect of capitalizing continues.
- Capitalizing an expenditure rather than expensing it results in greater amounts reported as cash from operations.
- If an asset is acquired in a nonmonetary exchange, its cost is based on the fair value of the asset given up, or the fair value of the asset acquired if it is more reliably determinable.
- Companies must capitalize interest costs associated with acquiring or constructing an asset that requires a long period of time to prepare for its intended use.
- Including capitalized interest in the calculation of interest coverage ratios provides a better assessment of a company's solvency.
- Generally, U.S. accounting standards require that research and development costs be expensed; however, certain costs related to software development are required to be capitalized. IFRS also require research costs be expensed but allows development costs to be capitalized under certain conditions.
- If companies apply different approaches to capitalizing software development costs, adjustments can be made to make the two comparable.
- When one company acquires another company, the transaction is accounted for using the purchase method of accounting in which the company identified as the acquirer allocates the purchase price to each asset acquired (and each liability assumed) on the basis of its fair value.
- Under purchase accounting, if the purchase price of an acquisition exceeds the sum of the amounts that can be allocated to individual assets and liabilities, the excess is recorded as goodwill.
- U.S. GAAP requires the immediate write-off of in-process R&D acquired in a business combination, but IFRS does not.
- Depreciation methods include: the straight-line method, in which the cost of an asset is allocated in equal amounts over its useful life; accelerated methods, in which the allocation of cost is greater in earlier years; and units-of-production methods, in which the allocation of cost corresponds to the actual use of an asset in a particular period.
- Significant estimates required for depreciation calculations include the useful life of the equipment (or its total lifetime productive capacity) and its expected residual value at the end of that useful life. A longer useful life and higher expected residual value decrease the amount of annual depreciation relative to a shorter useful life and lower expected residual value.

- Estimates of average age and remaining useful life of a company's assets reflect the relationship between assets accounted for on a historical cost basis and depreciation amounts.
- The average remaining useful life of a company's assets can be estimated as net PP&E divided by depreciation expense.
- To estimate the average age of the asset base, divide accumulated depreciation by depreciation expense.
- Intangible assets with finite useful lives are amortized over their useful lives.
- Intangible assets without a finite useful life, that is, with an indefinite useful life, are not amortized, but are reviewed for impairment whenever changes in events or circumstances indicate that the carrying amount of an asset may not be recoverable.
- For many types of long-lived tangible assets, ownership involves obligations that must be fulfilled at the end of the asset's service life, referred to as asset retirement obligations (AROs). Financial analysts often adjust financial statements to treat AROs in a manner consistent with debt.
- The gain or loss on the sale of long-lived assets is computed as the sales proceeds minus the carrying value of the asset at the time of sale.
- Long-lived assets to be disposed of other than by a sale—for example, abandoned, exchanged for another asset, or distributed to owners in a spin-off—are classified as held for use until disposal. Thus, they continue to be depreciated and tested for impairment.
- In contrast with depreciation and amortization charges, which serve to allocate the cost of a long-lived asset over its useful life, impairment charges reflect a decline in the fair value of an asset to an amount lower than its carrying value.
- Impairment disclosures can provide useful information about a company's expected cash flows.
- Under U.S. accounting standards, the value of long-lived assets is reported at depreciated historical cost. This value may be decreased by impairment charges, but cannot be increased. International accounting standards, however, permit impairment losses to be reversed, with the reversal reported in profit.

PROBLEMS

1. The Schneider Candy Company has decided to capitalize the interest costs it incurs during and related to construction of its new storage and shipping facility. This practice is
   A. permitted only if the company complies with U.S. GAAP.
   B. permitted only if the company complies with IFRS.
   C. permissible under either U.S. GAAP or IFRS.

2. The Juniper Juice Company reports that it has capitalized the interest costs it incurred during and related to construction of its new bottling plant. A creditor assessing Juniper Juice's solvency ratios would *most likely*
   A. add capitalized interest to reported interest expense.
   B. subtract capitalized interest from reported interest expense.
   C. add any depreciation from previously capitalized interest to interest expense.

3. Anna Lyssette is evaluating the performance of two biotechnology companies: Biotech Holdings and Advanced Biotech. Both companies released their first new drugs early in the year, but Lyssette is worried about a possible lack of comparability due to differing

strategies. Biotech Holdings acquired the research and development for its drug from another company while Advanced Biotech developed its drug internally. In the current accounting period, all else equal, Biotech Holdings would *most likely* report
A. lower total assets.
B. higher net income.
C. similar cash flow from operations.

4. Amerisoft complies with U.S. GAAP, while EuroWare complies with IFRS. When comparing the two companies, it would *most likely* be necessary to adjust the financial statements of
A. Amerisoft to remove charges related to acquired in-process R&D.
B. EuroWare to remove charges related to acquired in-process R&D.
C. Both companies to remove charges related to acquired in-process R&D.

5. When comparing a company that complies with IFRS to a company that complies with U.S. GAAP, it is *most* important to remember that under IFRS
A. research-phase R&D expenditures are capitalized.
B. acquired in-process R&D is expensed immediately.
C. development-phase R&D expenditures may be capitalized.

The following information relates to Problems 6 through 9:
The Asset Intensive Company (AIC) has purchased equipment for $1 million. The equipment is expected to have a three-year useful life and a salvage value of $100,000. AIC reports under U.S. GAAP.

6. Over the full life of the machine, all else equal, the volatility of AIC's net income will be
A. the same regardless of whether AIC expenses or capitalizes the cost of the machine.
B. highest if the company expenses the entire cost of the machine in the year of its purchase.
C. highest if the company capitalizes the cost of the machine and depreciates it over its useful life.

7. Assuming AIC capitalizes the cost of the equipment, depreciation expense over the life of the machine will be
A. the same regardless of the chosen depreciation method.
B. lowest if the company uses the double-declining balance method.
C. highest if the company uses the double-declining balance method.

8. In year 3, the return on equity will *most likely* be
A. highest if the company expenses the cost of the equipment.
B. highest if the company capitalizes the cost of the equipment.
C. the same regardless of whether the cost of the equipment is expensed or capitalized.

9. Regardless of the depreciation method used for reporting purposes, the company will use MACRS for tax purposes. In year 1, the reported income tax expense will be
A. the same regardless of depreciation method.
B. highest if the company uses the straight-line method.
C. highest if the company uses the double-declining balance method.

10. Bobcat Company's balance sheet shows PP&E valued at a historical cost of $22,983 million and accumulated depreciation of $7,879 million. Depreciation expense in the most recent year was $2,459 million. What is the average remaining useful life of Bobcat's assets?
    A. 3.2 years.
    B. 6.1 years.
    C. 9.3 years.

11. Francis Acana is comparing the property and equipment disclosures for three airline companies, as summarized in the following table:

	Airline A	Airline B	Airline C
Historical cost, aircraft	$17,239	£23,584	€45,266
Accumulated depreciation, aircraft	6,584	13,654	21,745
Net cost, aircraft	10,655	9,930	23,521
Annual depreciation expense	575	786	1,509

    Acana finds that the average fleet age is
    A. lowest for Airline A.
    B. lowest for Airline B.
    C. lowest for Airline C.

12. Relative to assets with finite lives, an intangible asset determined to have an indefinite life will result in lower reported
    A. assets.
    B. net income.
    C. amortization expense.

13. With regard to intangible assets, a company's reported profit margin the year the asset is acquired will be highest if it estimates a
    A. six-year useful life and no salvage value.
    B. six-year useful life and a positive salvage value.
    C. five-year useful life and a positive salvage value.

14. With regard to intangible assets, the company's cash flow from operating activities the year the asset is acquired will *most likely* be highest if it estimates a
    A. five-year useful life and no salvage value.
    B. six-year useful life and a positive salvage value.
    C. five-year useful life and a positive salvage value.

15. When a company is able to estimate the future costs it will incur when an asset is retired, it is *least likely* to
    A. increase the carrying value of the asset.
    B. decrease the carrying value of the liability through an accretion charge.
    C. decrease the carrying value of the asset over time through an accretion charge.

16. Compared to an asset that will not require a retirement obligation, an asset that will require a retirement obligation is *most likely* to result in a
    A. one-time charge at the time of retirement.
    B. rising debt/equity ratio as the retirement date approaches.
    C. declining debt/equity ratio as the retirement date approaches.

17. A credit analyst reviewing a company with asset retirement obligations (ARO) would *least likely* adjust
    A. interest expense by the amount of accretion.
    B. shareholders' equity by the amount of the ARO.
    C. the reported ARO by the amount of any related trust funds or escrow.

18. Fisherman Enterprises purchased $1 million of equipment with an estimated 10-year useful life and a $100,000 expected salvage value. The company uses the straight-line method of depreciation. At the end of five years it sells the equipment for $500,000. Fisherman's income statement will include a $50,000
    A. loss recorded as a separate line item.
    B. gain recorded as a separate line item.
    C. offset to depreciation and amortization.

19. A company that has decided to sell an asset is *least likely* to record a
    A. gain at the time the asset is sold.
    B. loss at the time the decision is made.
    C. gain at the time the decision is made.

20. An asset is considered impaired when
    A. its fair value exceeds its carrying value.
    B. its carrying value exceeds its fair value.
    C. it ceases to provide an economic benefit.

21. An asset impairment is *most likely* to impact reported
    A. depreciation expense in future periods.
    B. depreciation expense in the year impaired.
    C. cash flow from operating activities in the year impaired.

22. When comparing the reported results of a company that complies with U.S. GAAP to a company that complies with IFRS, return on assets is *least likely* to require an adjustment for
    A. goodwill amortization.
    B. upwardly revalued assets.
    C. acquired in-process R&D charges.

23. In the year of the revaluation, an asset revaluation that increases the carrying value of an asset is *most likely* to
    A. increase return on equity.
    B. decrease reported leverage.
    C. decrease shareholders' equity.

CHAPTER 12

INCOME TAXES

Elbie Antonites, CFA
University of Pretoria
Pretoria, South Africa

Michael A. Broihahn, CFA
Barry University
Miami, Florida

LEARNING OUTCOMES

After completing this chapter, you will be able to do the following:

- Explain the differences between accounting profit and taxable income, and define key terms including deferred tax assets, deferred tax liabilities, valuation allowance, taxes payable, and income tax expense.
- Explain how deferred tax liabilities and assets are created and the factors that determine how a company's deferred tax liabilities and assets should be treated for the purposes of financial analysis.
- Determine the tax base of a company's assets and liabilities.
- Calculate income tax expense, income taxes payable, deferred tax assets and deferred tax liabilities, and calculate and interpret the adjustment to the financial statements related to a change in the income tax rate.
- Evaluate the impact of tax rate changes on a company's financial statements and ratios.
- Distinguish between temporary and permanent items in pretax financial income and taxable income.
- Discuss the implications of a valuation allowance for deferred tax assets (i.e., when it is required, what impact it has on financial statements, and how it might affect an analyst's view of a company).
- Compare and contrast a company's deferred tax items and effective tax rate reconciliation between reporting periods.

- Analyze disclosures relating to deferred tax items and the effective tax rate reconciliation, and discuss how information included in these disclosures affects a company's financial statements and financial ratios.
- Identify the key provisions of and differences between income tax accounting under International Financial Reporting Standards (IFRS) and U.S. generally accepted accounting principles (U.S. GAAP).

SUMMARY OVERVIEW

Income taxes are a significant category of expense for profitable companies. Analyzing income tax expenses is often difficult for the analyst because there are many permanent and temporary timing differences between the accounting that is used for income tax reporting and the accounting that is used for financial reporting on company financial statements. The financial statements and notes to the financial statements of a company provide important information that the analyst needs to assess financial performance and to compare a company's financial performance with other companies. Key concepts in this chapter are as follows:

- Differences between the recognition of revenue and expenses for tax and accounting purposes may result in taxable income differing from accounting profit. The discrepancy is a result of different treatments of certain income and expenditure items.
- The tax base of an asset is the amount that will be deductible for tax purposes as an expense in the calculation of taxable income as the company expenses the tax basis of the asset. If the economic benefit will not be taxable, the tax base of the asset will be equal to the carrying amount of the asset.
- The tax base of a liability is the carrying amount of the liability less any amounts that will be deductible for tax purposes in the future. With respect to revenue received in advance, the tax base of such a liability is the carrying amount less any amount of the revenue that will not be taxable in future.
- Temporary differences arise from recognition of differences in the tax base and carrying amount of assets and liabilities. The creation of a deferred tax asset or liability as a result of a temporary difference will only be allowed if the difference reverses itself at some future date and to the extent that it is expected that the balance sheet item will create future economic benefits for the company.
- Permanent differences result in a difference in tax and financial reporting of revenue (expenses) that will not be reversed at some future date. Because it will not be reversed at a future date, these differences do not constitute temporary differences and do not give rise to a deferred tax asset or liability.
- Current taxes payable or recoverable are based on the applicable tax rates on the balance sheet date of an entity; in contrast, deferred taxes should be measured at the tax rate that is expected to apply when the asset is realized or the liability settled.
- All unrecognized deferred tax assets and liabilities must be reassessed on the appropriate balance sheet date and measured against their probable future economic benefit.
- Deferred tax assets must be assessed for their prospective recoverability. If it is probable that they will not be recovered at all or partly, the carrying amount should be reduced through the use of a deferred asset valuation allowance.

PROBLEMS

1. Using the straight-line method of depreciation for reporting purposes and accelerated depreciation for tax purposes would *most likely* result in a
   A. valuation allowance.
   B. deferred tax liability.
   C. temporary difference.

2. In early 2009 Sanborn Company must pay the tax authority €37,000 on the income it earned in 2008. This amount was recorded on the company's 31 December 2008 financial statements as
   A. taxes payable.
   B. income tax expense.
   C. a deferred tax liability.

3. Income tax expense reported on a company's income statement equals taxes payable, plus the net increase in
   A. deferred tax assets and deferred tax liabilities.
   B. deferred tax assets, less the net increase in deferred tax liabilities.
   C. deferred tax liabilities, less the net increase in deferred tax assets.

4. Analysts should treat deferred tax liabilities that are expected to reverse as
   A. equity.
   B. liabilities.
   C. neither liabilities nor equity.

5. Deferred tax liabilities should be treated as equity when
   A. they are not expected to reverse.
   B. the timing of tax payments is uncertain.
   C. the amount of tax payments is uncertain.

6. When both the timing and amount of tax payments is uncertain, analysts should treat deferred tax liabilities as
   A. equity.
   B. liabilities.
   C. neither liabilities nor equity.

7. When accounting standards require recognition of an expense that is not permitted under tax laws, the result is a
   A. deferred tax liability.
   B. temporary difference.
   C. permanent difference.

8. When certain expenditures result in tax credits that directly reduce taxes, the company will *most likely* record
   A. a deferred tax asset.
   B. a deferred tax liability.
   C. no deferred tax asset or liability.

9. When accounting standards require an asset to be expensed immediately but tax rules require the item to be capitalized and amortized, the company will *most likely* record
   A. a deferred tax asset.
   B. a deferred tax liability.
   C. no deferred tax asset or liability.

10. A company incurs a capital expenditure that may be amortized over five years for accounting purposes, but over four years for tax purposes. The company will *most likely* record
    A. a deferred tax asset.
    B. a deferred tax liability.
    C. no deferred tax asset or liability.

11. A company receives advance payments from customers that are immediately taxable but will not be recognized for accounting purposes until the company fulfills its obligation. The company will *most likely* record
    A. a deferred tax asset.
    B. a deferred tax liability.
    C. no deferred tax asset or liability.

Use the following disclosure related to income taxes to answer Problems 12–14.

NOTE I
Income Taxes
The components of earnings before income taxes are as follows ($ thousands):

	2007	2006	2005
Earnings before income taxes:			
United States	$88,157	$75,658	$59,973
Foreign	116,704	113,509	94,760
Total	$204,861	$189,167	$154,733

The components of the provision for income taxes are as follows ($ thousands):

	2007	2006	2005
Income taxes			
Current:			
Federal	$30,632	$22,031	$18,959
Foreign	28,140	27,961	22,263
	$58,772	$49,992	$41,222
Deferred:			
Federal	($4,752)	$5,138	$2,336
Foreign	124	1,730	621
	(4,628)	6,868	2,957
Total	$54,144	$56,860	$44,179

12. In 2007, the company's U.S. GAAP income statement recorded a provision for income taxes *closest* to
    A. $30,632.
    B. $54,144.
    C. $58,772.

13. The company's effective tax rate was *highest* in
    A. 2005.
    B. 2006.
    C. 2007.

14. Compared to the company's effective tax rate on U.S. income, its effective tax rate on foreign income was
    A. lower in each year presented.
    B. higher in each year presented.
    C. higher in some periods and lower in others.

15. Zimt AG presents its financial statements in accordance with International Financial Reporting Standards. In 2007, Zimt discloses a valuation allowance of €1,101 against total deferred tax assets of €19,201. In 2006, Zimt disclosed a valuation allowance of €1,325 against total deferred tax assets of €17,325. The change in the valuation allowance *most likely* indicates that Zimt's
    A. deferred tax liabilities were reduced in 2007.
    B. expectations of future earning power has increased.
    C. expectations of future earning power has decreased.

16. Cinnamon, Inc. recorded a total deferred tax asset in 2007 of $12,301, offset by a $12,301 valuation allowance. Cinnamon *most likely*
    A. fully utilized the deferred tax asset in 2007.
    B. has an equal amount of deferred tax assets and deferred tax liabilities.
    C. expects not to earn any taxable income before the deferred tax asset expires.

Use the following income tax disclosure to answer Problems 17–19.
    The tax effects of temporary differences that give rise to deferred tax assets and liabilities are as follows ($ thousands):

	2007	**2006**
Deferred tax assets:		
Accrued expenses	$8,613	$7,927
Tax credit and net operating loss carryforwards	2,288	2,554
LIFO and inventory reserves	5,286	4,327
Other	2,664	2,109
Deferred tax assets	18,851	16,917
Valuation allowance	(1,245)	(1,360)
Net deferred tax assets	$17,606	$15,557

	2007	2006
Deferred tax liabilities:		
Depreciation and amortization	(27,338)	(29,313)
Compensation and retirement plans	(3,831)	(8,963)
Other	(1,470)	(764)
Deferred tax liabilities	(32,639)	(39,040)
Net deferred tax liability	($15,033)	($23,483)

17. A reduction in the statutory tax rate would *most likely* benefit the company's
    A. income statement and balance sheet.
    B. income statement but not the balance sheet.
    C. balance sheet but not the income statement.

18. If the valuation allowance had been the same in 2007 as it was in 2006, the company
    would have reported $115 *higher*
    A. net income.
    B. deferred tax asset.
    C. income tax expense.

19. Compared to the provision for income taxes in 2007, the company's cash tax payments
    were
    A. lower.
    B. higher.
    C. the same.

Use the following income tax disclosure to answer Problems 20–22.
   A company's provision for income taxes resulted in effective tax rates attributable to loss
from continuing operations before cumulative effect of change in accounting principles that
varied from the statutory federal income tax rate of 34 percent, as summarized in the table
below.

Year ended 30 June	2007	2006	2005
Expected federal income tax expense (benefit) from continuing operations at 34 percent	($112,000)	$768,000	$685,000
Expenses not deductible for income tax purposes	357,000	32,000	51,000
State income taxes, net of federal benefit	132,000	22,000	100,000
Change in valuation allowance for deferred tax assets	(150,000)	(766,000)	(754,000)
Income tax expense	$227,000	$56,000	$82,000

20. In 2007, the company's net income (loss) was *closest* to
    A. ($217,000).
    B. ($329,000).
    C. ($556,000).

21. The $357,000 adjustment in 2007 *most likely* resulted in
    A. an increase in deferred tax assets.
    B. an increase in deferred tax liabilities.
    C. no change to deferred tax assets and liabilities.

22. Over the three years presented, changes in the valuation allowance for deferred tax assets were *most likely* indicative of
    A. decreased prospect for future profitability.
    B. increased prospects for future profitability.
    C. assets being carried at a higher value than their tax base.

CHAPTER 13

LONG-TERM LIABILITIES AND LEASES

Elizabeth A. Gordon

Temple University
Philadelphia, Pennsylvania

Elaine Henry, CFA

University of Miami
Coral Gables, Florida

LEARNING OUTCOMES

After completing this chapter, you will be able to do the following:

- Compute the effects of debt issuance and amortization of bond discounts and premiums on financial statements and ratios.
- Explain the role of debt covenants in protecting creditors by restricting a company's ability to invest, pay dividends, or make other operating and strategic decisions.
- Describe the presentation of, and disclosures relating to, financing liabilities.
- Determine the effects of changing interest rates on the market value of debt and on financial statements and ratios.
- Describe two types of debt with equity features (convertible debt and debt with warrants) and calculate the effect of issuance of such instruments on a company's debt ratios.
- Discuss the motivations for leasing assets instead of purchasing them and the incentives for reporting the leases as operating leases rather than finance leases.
- Determine the effects of finance and operating leases on the financial statements and ratios of the lessees and lessors.
- Distinguish between a sales-type lease and a direct financing lease, and determine the effects on the financial statements and ratios of the lessors.

- Describe the types and economic consequences of off-balance-sheet financing, and determine how take-or-pay contracts, throughput arrangements, and the sale of receivables affect financial statements and selected financial ratios.

SUMMARY OVERVIEW

Key points include the following:

- The sales proceeds of a bond issue are determined by discounting future cash payments using the market rate of interest. The reported interest expense on bonds is based on the market interest rate.
- Future cash payments on bonds usually include periodic interest payments (made at the stated rate) and the principal amount at maturity.
- When the market rate of interest is the stated rate for the bonds, the bonds will sell at par (i.e., at a price equal to the face value). When the market rate of interest is higher than the bonds' stated rate, the bonds will sell at a discount. When the market rate of interest is lower than the bonds' stated rate, the bonds will sell at a premium.
- An issuer amortizes any issuance discount or premium on bonds over the life of the bonds.
- If a company redeems bonds before maturity, it may show a gain or loss on debt extinguishment computed as the net book value of the bonds (including bond issuance costs under IFRS) less the amount required to redeem the bonds.
- Debt covenants impose restrictions on borrowers such as limitations on future borrowing or requirements to maintain a minimum debt-to-equity ratio.
- The book value of bonds is based on the face value adjusted for any unamortized discount or premium, which can differ from its fair value. Such a difference will be due to the implicit discount rate, established at the time of issue, being different from the current market rate.
- Under U.S. GAAP, convertible bonds, which allow bondholders to convert the bonds to equity, are reported at issuance with no separate value attributed to the conversion feature. IFRS separates the debt from the conversion feature, which is reported as equity.
- Bonds with warrants giving the holder the right to purchase additional shares of the issuer's common stock are reported at issuance with the issue proceeds allocated between the bonds and the warrants.
- Some financial instruments have characteristics of both debt and equity. If the financial instruments are treated as equity, solvency ratios based on the financial statements appear stronger.
- Accounting standards generally define two types of leases: operating leases and finance (or capital) leases. U.S. accounting standards have four specific requirements that define when a lease is a finance lease. International standards are less prescriptive.
- When a lessee reports a lease as an operating lease rather than a finance lease, it usually appears more profitable in early years of the lease and less so later, and it appears more solvent over the whole period.
- When a company has a substantial amount of operating leases, adjusting reported financials to include the impact of capitalizing these leases better reflects the company's solvency position.
- When a lessor reports a lease as a finance lease rather than an operating lease, it usually appears more profitable in early years of the lease.

- In direct financing leases, a lessor earns only interest revenue. In a sales-types lease, a lessor earns both interest revenue and a profit (or loss) on the sale of the leased asset.
- Companies can engage in other types of off-balance-sheet arrangements to avoid reporting additional liabilities on the balance sheet such as take-or-pay contracts, throughput arrangements, and the sale of receivables. Analysis should assess the impact on financial statements and financial ratios of adjustments reflecting the economic reality of off-balance-sheet financing activities.

PROBLEMS

1. A company issues $1 million of bonds at face value. When the bonds are issued, the company will record a
   A. cash inflow from investing activities.
   B. cash inflow from financing activities.
   C. cash inflow from operating activities.

2. Alpha Aircraft receives $1 million for bonds issued at face value, and Beta Bizjets receives $1 million for bonds issued at a discount. As a result of the bond issue, compared to Alpha Aircraft, Beta Bizjets will *most likely* record higher
   A. periodic interest expense on the income statement.
   B. liabilities on the balance sheet at the time of issue.
   C. periodic interest payments on the cash flow statement.

3. Oil Exploration LLC paid $45,000 related to printing, legal fees, commissions, and other costs associated with its recent bond issue. Under U.S. GAAP it is most likely to record these costs on its financial statements as
   A. an asset.
   B. a liability.
   C. a cash outflow from investing activities.

4. On 1 January 2008, Elegant Fragrances Company issues $1 million worth of five-year bonds with annual interest payments of $55,000 paid each 31 December. The market interest rate is 6.0 percent. Using the effective interest rate method of amortizing, Elegant Fragrances is *most likely* to record
   A. interest expense of $55,000 on its 2008 income statement.
   B. a liability of $982,674 on the 31 December 2008 balance sheet.
   C. a $58,736 cash outflow from operating activity on the 2008 statement of cash flows.

5. Consolidated Enterprises issues $10 million worth of five-year bonds with a stated rate of 6.5 percent at a time when the market interest rate is 6.0 percent. Using the effective interest rate method of amortizing, the carrying value after one year will be *closest to*
   A. $10.17 million.
   B. $10.21 million.
   C. $10.28 million.

6. Innovative Inventions, Inc. needs to raise $10 million and typically would issue coupon-bearing bonds at par value. If the company chooses to issue zero-coupon bonds instead, its debt-to-equity ratio will
   A. rise as the maturity date approaches.
   B. decline as the maturity date approaches.
   C. remain constant throughout the life of the bond.

7. Fairmont Golf issued fixed rate debt when interest rates were 6 percent. Rates have since risen to 7 percent. Using the values reported on the financial statements would *most likely* cause an analyst to
   A. overestimate Fairmont's economic liabilities.
   B. underestimate Fairmont's economic liabilities.
   C. underestimate Fairmont's interest coverage ratio.

8. Debt covenants are *least likely* to place restrictions on the issuer's ability to
   A. pay dividends.
   B. issue additional debt.
   C. issue additional equity.

9. Sheila Cummins is analyzing the financial statements of a company that has issued convertible bonds that are currently reported as debt. Cummins is considering potential adjustments to the debt-to-equity ratio as part of her analysis. The *least appropriate* action would be to
   A. make no adjustment.
   B. adjust debt but not equity.
   C. adjust equity but not debt.

10. Why-Fi Incorporated reports total equity of $10 million. It has also issued convertible bonds with a book value of $10 million that are convertible into equity with a current market value of $15 million. Under U.S. GAAP, if the bonds are converted, Why-Fi will report total equity *closest to*
    A. $10 million.
    B. $20 million.
    C. $25 million.

11. When analyzing the financial statements of Energy Resources, Inc., Frederico Montalban, CFA, is treating its convertible bonds issue as equity rather than debt. Montalban's analysis is *most likely* appropriate
    A. if the conversion price is near the current market price of the stock.
    B. if the conversion price is significantly above the current market price of the stock.
    C. if the conversion price is significantly below the current market price of the stock.

12. Capitol Services Corp. has $300 million in shareholders' equity and $400 million in long-term debt, of which $200 million are convertible bonds. What would Capitol's long-term debt-to-equity ratio be if the bonds were converted?
    A. 0.40
    B. 0.80
    C. 0.67

13. Assets that are being used under a synthetic lease are reported as though the lessee owns them
    A. for tax purposes and on the financial statements.
    B. on the financial statements but not for tax purposes.
    C. for tax purposes but not on the financial statements.

14. Compared to using a finance lease, a lessee that makes use of an operating lease will report higher
    A. debt.
    B. rent expense.
    C. cash flow from operating activity.

15. The notes to the financial statements of Bargain Apparel Corp. disclose that the company has finance lease commitments with minimum future payments of $20 million, of which $6 million represents interest payments. It also has operating leases with minimum future payments of $25 million. If Robert Xu, CFA, wishes to adjust the financial statements to treat all leases as debt, he should increase reported total liabilities by an amount *closest to*
    A. $17.5 million.
    B. $25.0 million.
    C. $45.0 million.

16. Compared to an identical company that uses an operating lease, a company that uses a finance lease will *most likely* produce a reported return on equity (ROE) that
    A. starts lower but rises during the life of the lease.
    B. starts higher but decline during the life of the lease.
    C. starts lower and remains so during the life of the lease.

17. For a lessor, the leased asset appears on the balance sheet and continues to be depreciated when the lease is classified as
    A. a sales-type lease.
    B. an operating lease.
    C. a direct financing lease.

18. A lessor's reported revenues at lease inception will be *highest* if the lease is classified as
    A. a sales-type lease.
    B. an operating lease.
    C. a direct financing lease.

19. The lessor will record interest income if the lease is classified as
    A. sales-type only.
    B. direct financing only.
    C. either sales-type or direct financing.

20. Cavalier Copper Mines has $840 million in total liabilities and $520 million in shareholders' equity. It has disclosed $100 million in purchase commitments over the next

five years. An analyst wishing to treat the purchase commitments as debt would calculate a debt to total capital ratio *closest to*

A. 0.58.

B. 0.59.

C. 0.64.

21. Charles McKimmon, CFA, is analyzing the financial statements of Computers On Credit, Inc. (COC). COC has sold $60 million of accounts receivable for proceeds of $50 million, and McKimmon wishes to treat the transaction as collateralized borrowing. McKimmon's financial statement adjustments will *most likely* include adding

A. $50 million to accounts receivable.

B. $50 million to cash flows from financing activity.

C. $50 million to cash flows from operating activity.

CHAPTER 14

EMPLOYEE COMPENSATION: POSTRETIREMENT AND SHARE-BASED

Elaine Henry, CFA

University of Miami
Coral Gables, Florida

Elizabeth A. Gordon

Temple University
Philadelphia, Pennsylvania

LEARNING OUTCOMES

After completing this chapter, you will be able to do the following:

- Explain the types of postretirement benefit plans and the implications for financial reports.
- Explain the measures of a defined-benefit pension plan's liabilities, including the projected benefit obligation, accumulated benefit obligation, and vested benefit obligation.
- Describe the components of a company's defined-benefit pension expense and explain the impact of plan assumptions on that pension expense.
- Explain the impact on financial statements of International Financial Reporting Standards (IFRS) and U.S. generally accepted accounting principles (U.S. GAAP) for pension and other postretirement benefits that permit some items to be reported in the footnotes rather than being reflected in the financial statements themselves.
- Evaluate pension plan footnote disclosures, including cash flow–related information.

- Evaluate the underlying economic liability (or asset) of a company based upon pension and other postretirement benefit disclosures.
- Calculate the underlying economic pension and other postretirement expense (income) based on disclosures.
- Discuss the main issues involved in accounting for share-based compensation.
- Explain the impact on financial statements of accounting for stock grants and stock options, and the importance of companies' assumptions in valuing these grants and options.

SUMMARY OVERVIEW

This chapter discusses two different forms of employee compensation: postretirement benefits and share-based compensation. While different, the two share similarities in that they are forms of compensation outside of the standard salary arrangements. They also involve complex valuation, accounting, and reporting issues. While U.S. GAAP and IFRS are converging on accounting and reporting, it is important to note that differences in a country's social system, laws, and regulations can result in differences in a company's pension and share-based compensation plans that may be reflected in the company's earnings and financial reports.

Key points include the following:

- Defined-contribution pension plans specify only the amount of contribution to the plan; the eventual amount of the pension benefit to the employee will depend on the value of an employee's plan assets at the time of retirement.
- Defined-benefit pension plans specify the amount of the pension benefit, often determined by a plan formula, under which the eventual amount of the benefit to the employee is a function of length of service and final salary.
- Differences exist in countries' regulatory requirements for companies to fund DB pension plan obligations.
- DB pension plan obligations are funded by the sponsoring company contributing assets to a pension trust, a separate legal entity.
- Three measures are used in estimating a DB pension plan's liabilities, each increasingly more inclusive: the vested benefit obligation, the accumulated benefit obligation, and the projected benefit obligation.
- For analysis, the projected benefit obligation is typically the most appropriate measure because it recognizes future salary increases.
- Balance sheet reporting is less relevant for DC plans because companies make contributions to DC plans as the expense arises and thus no liabilities accrue for that type of plan.
- IFRS requires companies' balance sheets to reflect as a DB liability the pension obligation minus the fair value of plan assets, with certain adjustments for actuarial gains or losses, and any past service costs not yet recognized.
- New U.S. accounting standards require that companies' balance sheets reflect as a DB liability the pension obligation minus the fair value of plan sets, with no further adjustments.
- Because the IASB and the FASB have identified pensions and postretirement benefit accounting as a major area for collaborative efforts, the new U.S. accounting standards are also relevant for anticipating future changes for companies using IFRS.
- Pension expense includes the following components: service cost, interest expense, prior service cost, actuarial gains and losses, and return on plan assets (which reduces pension expense).

- Estimates of the future obligation under DB pension plans and other postretirement benefits are sensitive to numerous assumptions, including discount rates, assumed annual compensation increases, expected return on plan assets, and assumed health care cost inflation.
- Employee compensation packages are structured to fulfill varied objectives including satisfying employees' needs for liquidity, retaining employees, and providing incentives to employees.
- Common components of employee compensation packages are salary, bonuses, and share-based compensation.
- Share-based compensation serves to align employees' interest with those of the shareholders. It includes stocks and stock options.
- Share-based compensation has the advantage of requiring no current-period cash outlays.
- Share-based compensation is reported at fair value under U.S. GAAP and IFRS.
- The valuation technique, or option pricing model, that the company uses is an important choice in determining fair value and is disclosed.
- Key assumptions and input into option pricing models include items such as exercise price, stock price volatility, estimated life of each award, estimated number of options that will be forfeited, and the risk-free rate of interest. Certain assumptions are highly subjective, such as stock price volatility or the expected life of stock options, and can greatly change the estimated fair value and thus compensation expense.

PROBLEMS

The following information relates to Problems 1 through 6.

Magenta Corp. is based in the United States and offers its employees a defined-benefit pension plan. The company's effective tax rate for 2008 is 40 percent. Excerpts from a financial statement footnote on Magenta's retirement plans are presented in Exhibit 14-1.

EXHIBIT 14-1   Magenta Corp. Defined-Benefit Pension Plan

($ millions)	2008
Change in benefit obligation	
Benefit obligations at beginning of year	$28,416
Service cost	96
Interest cost	1,557
Actuarial (gains) losses	−306
Prior service costs	132
Foreign exchange impact	−42
Benefits paid	−1,332
Benefit obligations at end of year	$28,531
Change in plan assets	
Fair value of plan assets at beginning of year	$23,432
Actual return on plan assets	1,302
Employer contributions	693
Benefits paid	−1,332
Fair value of plan assets at end of year	$24,105

(*Continued*)

EXHIBIT 14-1   (*Continued*)

($ millions)	2008
Components of net periodic benefit cost	
Service cost	$96
Interest cost	1,557
Expected return plan assets	−1,874
Amortization of net actuarial loss	264
Net periodic benefit cost	$43

1. At year-end 2008, $28,531 represents the defined benefit pension plan's
   A. vested benefit obligation.
   B. projected benefit obligation.
   C. accumulated benefit obligation.

2. The economic pension expense for Magenta's DB plan is *closest to*
   A. $135 million
   B. $1,251 million
   C. $2,509 million

3. The difference between Magenta's estimated economic pension expense for the period
   and the reported pension expense is *closest to*
   A. $92 million
   B. $1,208 million
   C. $1,302 million

4. To adjust Magenta's reported net income to reflect the company's underlying economic
   pension expense, an analyst would decrease net income by an amount *closest to*
   A. $43 million.
   B. $55 million.
   C. $135 million.

5. In order to reflect the underlying economic liability of Magenta's defined-benefit pension
   plan, an analyst would adjust Magenta's 2008 balance sheet to include a $24,105
   A. increase in assets and equity.
   B. increase in assets and liabilities.
   C. increase in liabilities and reduction to equity.

6. An adjustment to the Magenta's statement of cash flows to reclassify the company's excess
   contribution for 2008 would *most likely* entail reclassifying $558 million as an outflow
   related to
   A. investing activities rather than operating activities
   B. financing activities rather than operating activities
   C. operating activities rather than financing activities

The following information relates to Problems 7 through 12.
   Passaic Industries is based in the United States and offers its employees both a defined-
benefit pension plan and stock options. Several of the disclosures related to these plans are
presented in Exhibits 14-2, 14-3, and 14-4.

EXHIBIT 14-2   Components of Expense (Income)

	Year Ended 31 December		
	2008	**2007**	**2006**
Components of expense/(income)			
Service cost	$908	$910	$831
Interest cost	2,497	2,457	2,378
Expected return on plan assets	(3,455)	(3,515)	(3,378)
Amortization of prior service costs	188	185	180
Recognized net actuarial loss/(gain)	912	1,266	440
Net periodic benefit cost	$1,050	$1,303	$451

EXHIBIT 14-3   Funded Status of Plan

At 31 December ($ millions)	2008	2007
Change in benefit obligation		
Beginning balance	$45,183	$42,781
Service cost	908	910
Interest cost	2,497	2,457
Plan participants' contributions	9	12
Amendments	156	270
Actuarial (gain)/loss	(925)	2,778
Settlement/curtailment/acquisitions/dispositions, net	85	(1,774)
Benefits paid	(2,331)	(2,251)
Ending balance	$45,582	$45,183
Change in plan assets		
Beginning balance at fair value	$43,484	$38,977
Actual return on plan assets	4,239	5,460
Company contribution	526	2,604
Plan participants' contributions	9	12
Settlement/curtailment/acquisitions/dispositions, net	216	(1,393)
Benefits paid	(2,286)	(2,208)
Exchange rate adjustment	15	32
Ending balance at fair value	$46,203	$43,484

EXHIBIT 14-4   Volatility Assumptions Used to Value Stock Option Grants

Grant Year	Weighted Average Expected Volatility
2008 valuation assumptions	
2004–2008	21.50%
2007 valuation assumptions	
2003–2007	23.00%

7. With regard to its defined-benefit pension plan, Passaic's year-end 2008 balance sheet *most likely* presents a
   A. $621 million asset.
   B. $621 million liability.
   C. $1,699 million liability.

8. The pension expense reported on the Passaic Industries income statement for the year ending 31 December 2008 is *closest* to
   A. $908 million.
   B. $1,050 million.
   C. $2,331 million.

9. The Passaic Industries statement of cash flows for the year ended 31 December 2008 shows the reconciliation of net income to cash flows from operating activities for the period. The associated adjustment to net income related to the DB plan is *closest* to
   A. $526 million.
   B. $2,331 million.
   C. $4,239 million.

10. The estimated increase in the pension obligation due to benefits earned by current employees in 2008 is *closest* to
    A. $908 million.
    B. $1,050 million.
    C. $2,331 million.

11. Because of the changes in pension plan assets and benefit obligations reported in the Funded Status of Plan reported at 31 December 2007 and 31 December 2008, the 2008 Passaic Industries balance sheet compared to the 2007 balance sheet will show a $2,320 increase in
    A. assets.
    B. liabilities.
    C. shareholders' equity.

12. Compared to 2008 net income as reported, if Passaic Industries had used the same expected volatility assumption for its 2008 option grants that it had used in 2007, its 2008 net income would have been
    A. lower.
    B. higher.
    C. the same.

The following information relates to Problems 13 through 18.
   Stereo Warehouse is a U.S. retailer that offers employees a defined-benefit pension plan and stock options as part of its compensation package. Peter Friedland, CFA, is an equity analyst concerned with earnings quality. He is particularly interested in whether the discretionary assumptions the company is making regarding compensation plans are contributing to the recent earnings growth at Stereo Warehouse. He gathers information from the company's regulatory filings regarding the pension plan assumptions in Exhibit 14-5, the actual asset allocation for the pension plan in Exhibit 14-6, and the assumptions related to option valuation in Exhibit 14-7.

EXHIBIT 14-5   Assumptions Used for Stereo Warehouse Defined-Benefit Plan

	2008	2007	2006
Expected long-term rate of return on plan assets	6.06%	6.14%	6.79%
Discount rate	4.85	4.94	5.38
Salary increases	4.00	4.44	4.25
Inflation	3.00	2.72	2.45

EXHIBIT 14-6   Allocation of Stereo Warehouse Defined-Benefit Plan Assets

	2008	2007
Equity securities	90%	80%
Debt securities	10	20

EXHIBIT 14-7   Option Valuation Assumptions

	2008	2007	2006
Risk free rate	4.6%	3.8%	2.4%
Expected life	5.0 yrs	4.5 yrs	5.0 yrs
Dividend yield	1.0%	0.0%	0.0%
Expected volatility	29%	31%	35%

13. Compared to the 2008 reported financial statements, if Stereo Warehouse had used the same expected long-term rate of return on plan assets assumption in 2008 as it used in 2006, its year-end 2008 pension obligation would *most likely* have been
   A. lower.
   B. higher.
   C. the same.

14. Compared to the reported 2008 financial statements, if Stereo Warehouse had used the same discount rate as it used in 2006, it would have *most likely* reported lower
   A. net income.
   B. total liabilities.
   C. cash flow from operating activities.

15. Compared to the assumptions Stereo Warehouse used to compute its pension expense in 2007, earnings in 2008 were *most favorably* impacted by the change in the
   A. discount rate.
   B. expected salary increases.
   C. expected long-term rate of return on plan assets.

16. The pension assumptions being used by Stereo Warehouse may be *internally inconsistent* with respect to
    A. asset returns only.
    B. inflation expectations only.
    C. both inflation expectations and asset returns.

17. Compared to the reported 2008 financial statements, if Stereo Warehouse had used the 2006 expected volatility assumption to value its employee stock options it would have *most likely* reported higher
    A. net income.
    B. compensation expense.
    C. deferred compensation liability.

18. Compared to the assumptions Stereo Warehouse used to value stock options in 2007, earnings in 2008 were most favorably impacted by the change in the
    A. expected life.
    B. risk-free rate.
    C. dividend yield.

The following information relates to Problems 19 through 24.

Andreas Kordt is an equity analyst examining the financial statements of Aero Euro. Aero Euro is based in Belgium and complies with IFRS. Kordt believes that the accounting guidelines for defined-benefit plans do not reflect the underlying economic financial conditions and he intends to adjust Aero Euro's financial statements accordingly. He also wants to compare the reported financial statements to those of a company that follows U.S. GAAP. As an initial step, he pulled certain information relating to the plans, which is presented in Exhibits 14-8 and 14-9.

EXHIBIT 14-8   Pension Plan Assumptions for Aero Euro

	2008	2007	2006
Discount rate	4.51%	4.49%	4.55%
Salary inflation rate	2.62%	2.70%	2.91%
Expected long-term rate of return on plan assets	5.70%	5.70%	5.13%

EXHIBIT 14-9   Information Related to Aero Euro's Defined-Benefit Plans

	Pension Benefits (€ millions)		
	2008	2007	2006
Benefit obligation at beginning of year	10,921	10,313	9,208
Service cost	368	359	275
Interest cost	489	461	447
Employees' contribution	40	36	32

	Pension Benefits(€ millions)		
	2008	**2007**	**2006**
Plan amendments	150	49	16
Settlements/curtailments	(28)	(11)	(1)
Benefits paid	(423)	(398)	(352)
Actuarial loss / (gain)	68	106	707
Currency translation adjustment	(3)	6	(19)
Benefit obligation at end of year	11,582	10,921	10,313
Fair value of plan assets at beginning of year	12,538	10,782	9,936
Actual return on plan assets	936	1,763	920
Employers' contributions	323	358	261
Employees' contributions	40	36	32
Settlements/curtailments	(6)	(6)	—
Benefits paid	(423)	(398)	(352)
Currency translation adjustment	(4)	3	(15)
Fair value of plan assets at end of year	13,404	12,538	10,782
Funded status	1,822	1,617	469
Unrecognized prior service cost	190	59	25
Unrecognized actuarial (gains) / losses	(857)	(710)	322
Prepaid (accrued) pension cost	1,155	966	816
Amounts recorded in the balance sheet:			
Pension asset	2,097	1,903	1,767
Provision for retirement benefits	(942)	(937)	(951)
Net amount recognized	1,155	966	816
Net periodic cost :			
Service cost	368	359	275
Interest cost	489	461	447
Expected return on plan assets	(714)	(616)	(532)
Settlement/curtailment	(18)	(8)	—
Amortization of prior service cost	19	12	15
Amortization of unrecognized actuarial (gain) loss	(1)	16	(4)
Other	—	(1)	—
Net periodic cost	143	223	201
Accumulated benefit obligation	10,018	9,656	9,081

19. At year-end 2008, €10,018 million represents the total present value of benefits Aero Euro's employees
    A. have earned to date.
    B. would receive if they left the company.
    C. are expected to earn during their career.

20. The adjustments Kordt needs to make in order to reflect the underlying economic pension expense for 2008 include subtracting
    A. €423 million from the change in benefit obligation.
    B. €423 million from the change in the value of plan assets.
    C. €323 million from the change in the value of plan assets.

21. The 2008 pension expense recognized on Aero Euro's income statement is *closest* to
    A. €143 million.
    B. €423 million.
    C. €1,155 million.

22. Adjusting Aero Euro's 2008 balance sheet to reflect the underlying economic position of the company's defined benefit plan would result in a €667 increase in
    A. assets.
    B. liabilities.
    C. shareholders' equity.

23. Compared to the reported 2008 financial statements, if Aero Euro used the 2006 salary inflation rate in 2008 it would have *most likely* reported higher
    A. net income.
    B. benefit obligation.
    C. amortization of prior service cost.

24. Compared to the reported 2008 financial statements, if Aero Euro used the 2006 expected long-term rate of return on plan assets in 2008 it would have *most likely* reported higher
    A. net assets.
    B. net income.
    C. pension expense.

CHAPTER 15

INTERCORPORATE INVESTMENTS

Susan Perry Williams

McIntire School of Commerce
University of Virginia
Charlottesville, Virginia

LEARNING OUTCOMES

After completing this chapter, you will be able to do the following:

- Explain the categorization of intercorporate investments into minority passive, minority active, joint ventures, and controlling interest.
- Describe the reporting under International Financial Reporting Standards (IFRS) and U.S. generally accepted accounting principles (U.S. GAAP) of the four categories of intercorporate investments including the use of different accounting methods: equity, proportionate consolidation, and consolidation; and including the treatment of goodwill.
- Contrast the purchase method, the pooling of interest method, and the acquisition method, used in business combinations and evaluate the impact of each method on reported financial results.
- Explain the implications on performance ratios of the different accounting methods used for intercorporate investments.
- Identify the accounting issues associated with special purpose entities (SPEs) or variable interest entities.

SUMMARY OVERVIEW

Intercompany investments play a significant role in business activities and create significant challenges for the analyst in assessing company performance. Investments in other corporations can take four basic forms: minority passive investments, minority active investments, joint ventures, and controlling interest investments. Key concepts are as follows:

- Minority passive investments are those in which the investor has no significant influence. They can be designated as: held-to-maturity investments, held-for-trading securities, or available-for-sale securities. Additionally, both IFRS and U.S GAAP allow investments to be designated at fair value. IFRS and U.S. GAAP treat minority passive investments in a similar manner.
  - Held-to-maturity investments are carried at cost.
  - Held-for-trading securities are carried at fair value; unrealized gains and losses are reported on the profit and loss (income) statement.
  - Available-for-sale securities are carried at fair value; unrealized gains and losses are reported in the statement of recognized income and expenses (IFRS) or other comprehensive income (U.S. GAAP) in the equity section of the balance sheet.
  - Gains or losses on investments designated as fair value are reported on the profit and loss (income) statement.
- Minority active investments are those in which the investor has significant influence, but not control, over the investee's business activities. Because the investor can exert significant influence over financial and operating policy decisions, the equity method of accounting provides a more objective basis for reporting investment income.
  - The equity method requires the investor to recognize income as earned rather than when dividends are received.
  - The equity investment is carried at cost, plus its share of post-acquisition income (after adjustments) less dividends received.
  - The equity investment is reported as a single line item on the balance sheet and on the income statement.
- Joint ventures are entities owned and operated by a small group of investors with shared common control. IFRS and U.S. GAAP apply different standards to joint ventures. IFRS favor proportionate consolidation that requires the venturer's share of the assets, liabilities, income, and expenses of the joint venture to be combined on a line-by-line basis with similar items in the venturer's financial statements. U.S. GAAP requires the equity method accounting for joint ventures. The IASB is expected to issue a statement that changes accounting for joint ventures from proportionate consolidation to the equity method.
- Controlling interests investments can be structured as mergers, acquisitions, or statutory consolidation.
- In a statutory merger, two or more companies combine such that only one of the companies remains in existence. In a statutory consolidation, two or more companies are folded into a new entity with the new entity becoming the surviving company.
- An acquisition allows for the legal continuity for each of the combining companies. Both companies continue as separate entities but are now affiliated through a parent–subsidiary relationship.
  - Unlike a statutory merger or consolidation, the acquiring company does not need to acquire 100 percent of the target. If the acquiring company acquires less than 100 percent, minority (noncontrolling) shareholders' interests are reported on the consolidated financial statements.
  - Consolidated financial statements are prepared in each reporting period.
- Current accounting standards (IFRS and U.S. GAAP) require the purchase method for business combinations. Fair value is the appropriate measurement for identifiable assets

and liabilities acquired in the business combination. If the acquisition is less than 100 percent, U.S. GAAP revalues only the portion of the company acquired, whereas IFRS revalue the total assets or liabilities. FASB (SFAS No. 141R), effective after 15 December 2008 and the soon to be released IASB revision of IFRS 3 (effective after 1 January 2009) will require the acquisition method for business combinations. Identifiable assets and liabilities will be measured at fair value.

- The pooling of interests method for business combinations was not allowed after June 2001 in U.S. GAAP (March 2004 in IFRS).
- Goodwill is the excess purchase price after recognizing the fair market value of all tangible and intangible assets acquired. U.S. GAAP (SFAS No. 141R) will also recognize goodwill for the noncontrolling interest (full goodwill), whereas the new IASB standard will provide the option for full or proportionate goodwill.
- Goodwill has an indefinite life and is not amortized but is evaluated at least annually for impairment. Impairment losses are reported on the income statement.
- Variable interests (SPEs) require consolidation with the sponsoring company if the sponsoring company bears the majority of risks and rewards from the transaction.
  - U.S. GAAP allows for qualified special purpose entities to avoid consolidation if the sponsoring company is not the primary beneficiary.

PROBLEMS

The following information relates to Problems 1 through 6.

Cinnamon, Inc. is a diversified manufacturing company headquartered in the United States, and it complies with U.S. GAAP. In 2008, Cinnamon held a 19 percent passive stake in Cambridge Processing that was classified as available for sale. During the year, the value of this stake rose by $2 million. In December 2008, Cinnamon announced that it would be increasing its ownership to 50 percent effective 1 January 2009.

Peter Lubbock, an analyst following both Cinnamon and Cambridge, is curious how the increased stake will affect Cinnamon's consolidated financial statements. He asks Cinnamon's chief financial officer how the company will account for the stake, and is told that the decision has not yet been made. Lubbock decides to use his existing forecasts for both companies' financial statements to compare various alternative outcomes.

Lubbock gathers abbreviated financial statement data for Cinnamon (Exhibit 15-1) and Cambridge (Exhibit 15-2) for this purpose.

EXHIBIT 15-1   Selected Financial Statement Estimates for Cinnamon, Inc. ($ millions)

Year ending 31 December	2008	2009[a]
Revenue	$1,400	$1,575
Operating income	126	142
Net income	62	69
Total assets	1,170	1,317
Shareholders' equity	616	685

[a]Estimates made prior to announcement of increased stake in Cambridge.

EXHIBIT 15-2   Selected Financial Statement Estimates for Cambridge
Processing ($ millions)

Year ending 31 December	2008	2009
Revenue	$1,000	$1,100
Operating income	80	88
Net income	40	44
Dividends paid	20	22
Total assets	800	836
Shareholders' equity	440	462

1. In 2008, Cinnamon's earnings before taxes includes a contribution (in $ millions) from
   its investment in Cambridge Processing *closest* to
   A. $2.5 million.
   B. $3.8 million.
   C. $5.0 million.

2. In 2009, Cinnamon is *least likely* to account for its investment in Cambridge under
   which of the following methods?
   A. Equity
   B. Purchase method
   C. Proportionate consolidation

3. On 31 December 2009, Cinnamon's shareholders' equity amount on the balance sheet
   would *most likely* be
   A. highest if Cinnamon is deemed to have control of Cambridge.
   B. independent of the accounting method used for the investment in Cambridge.
   C. highest if Cinnamon is deemed to have significant influence over Cambridge.

4. In 2009, Cinnamon's net profit margin would be *highest* if
   A. it is deemed to have control of Cambridge.
   B. it had not increased its stake in Cambridge.
   C. it is deemed to have significant influence over Cambridge.

5. On 31 December 2009, Cinnamon's reported debt-to-equity ratio will most likely be
   highest if it is deemed to have
   A. control of Cambridge.
   B. joint control of Cambridge.
   C. significant influence over Cambridge.

6. Compared to Cinnamon's operating margin in 2008, if it is deemed to have control of
   Cambridge, its operating margin in 2009 will *most likely* be
   A. lower.
   B. higher.
   C. the same.

The following information relates to Problems 7 through 12.

Zimt AG is a consumer products manufacturer headquartered in Austria. It complies with IFRS.

In 2008, Zimt held a 10 percent passive stake in Oxbow Limited that was classified as held-for-trading securities. During the year, the value of this stake declined by €3 million.

In December 2008, Zimt announced that it would be increasing its ownership to 50 percent effective 1 January 2009.

Franz Gelblum, an analyst following both Zimt and Oxbow, is curious how the increased stake will affect Zimt's consolidated financial statements. Because Gelblum is uncertain how the company will account for the increased stake, he uses his existing forecasts for both companies' financial statements to compare various alternative outcomes.

Gelblum gathers abbreviated financial statement data for Zimt (Exhibit 15-3) and Oxbow (Exhibit 15-4) for this purpose.

EXHIBIT 15-3   Selected Financial Statement Estimates for Zimt AG (€ millions)

Year ending 31 December	2008	2009
Revenue	€1,500	€1,700
Operating income	135	153
Net income	66	75
Total assets	1,254	1,421
Shareholders' equity	660	735

EXHIBIT 15-4   Selected Financial Statement Estimates for Oxbow Limited (€ millions)

Year ending 31 December	2008	2009
Revenue	€1,200	€1,350
Operating income	120	135
Net income	60	68
Dividends paid	20	22
Total assets	1,200	1,283
Shareholders' equity	660	706

7. In 2008, Zimt's earnings before taxes includes a contribution (in € millions) from its investment in Oxbow Limited *closest* to
   A. (€0.6) million.
   B. €1.0 million.
   C. €1.9 million.

8. On 31 December 2009, Zimt's total assets balance would *most likely* be
   A. highest if Zimt is deemed to have control of Oxbow.
   B. highest if Zimt is deemed to have significant influence over Oxbow.
   C. unaffected by the accounting method used for the investment in Oxbow.

9. Based on Gelblum's estimates, if Zimt is deemed to have significant influence over Oxbow, its 2009 operating income would be *closest* to
   A. €153.
   B. €221.
   C. €288.

10. Based on Gelblum's estimates, if Zimt is deemed to have joint control of Oxbow, and Zimt uses the proportionate consolidation method, its 31 December 2009 total liabilities will *most likely* be *closest* to
    A. €686.
    B. €975.
    C. €1,263.

11. Based on Gelblum's estimates, if Zimt is deemed to have control over Oxbow, its 2009 consolidated sales will be *closest* to
    A. €1,700.
    B. €2,375.
    C. €3,050.

12. Based on Gelblum's estimates, Zimt's net income in 2009 will *most likely* be
    A. highest if Zimt is deemed to have control of Oxbow.
    B. highest if Zimt is deemed to have significant influence over Oxbow.
    C. independent of the accounting method used for the investment in Oxbow.

The following information relates to Problems 13 through 18.

Burton Howard, CFA, is an equity analyst with Maplewood Securities. Howard is preparing a research report on Confabulated Materials, SA, a publicly traded company based in France that complies with IFRS. As part of his analysis, Howard has assembled data gathered from the financial statement footnotes of Confabulated's 2008 annual report and from discussions with company management. Howard is concerned about the effect of this information on Confabulated's future earnings.

Information about Confabulated's investment portfolio for the years ended 31 December 2007 and 2008 is presented in Exhibit 15-5. As part of his research, Howard is considering the possible effect on reported income of Confabulated's accounting classification for fixed income investments.

EXHIBIT 15-5   Confabulated's Investment Portfolio (€ thousands)

Characteristic	Bugle AG	Cathay Corp.	Dumas SA
Classification	Available-for-sale	Held-to-maturity	Held-to-maturity
Cost[a]	€25,000	€40,000	€50,000
Market value, 31 December 2007	29,000	38,000	54,000
Market value, 31 December 2008	28,000	37,000	55,000

[a]All securities were purchased at par value.

In addition, Confabulated's financial reports discuss a transaction under which receivables were factored through an SPE for Confabulated's benefit.

13. The balance sheet carrying value of Confabulated's investment portfolio (in € thousands) at 31 December 2008 is *closest* to
    A. 112,000.
    B. 115,000.
    C. 118,000.

14. The balance sheet carrying value of Confabulated's investment portfolio (in € thousands) at 31 December 2008 would have been higher if which of the securities had been reclassified as a held-for-trading security?
    A. Bugle.
    B. Cathay.
    C. Dumas.

15. Compared to Confabulated's reported interest income in 2009, if Dumas had been classified as available-for-sale, the interest income would have been
    A. lower.
    B. the same.
    C. higher.

16. Compared to Confabulated's reported earnings before taxes in 2009, if Bugle had been classified as a held-for-trading security, the earnings before taxes would have been
    A. the same.
    B. €1,000 lower.
    C. €3,000 higher.

17. Confabulated's reported interest income would be higher if the cost were the same but the par value of
    A. Bugle was €28,000.
    B. Cathay was €37,000.
    C. Dumas was €55,000.

18. Confabulated's special purpose entity is *most likely* to be
    A. held off balance sheet.
    B. consolidated on Confabulated's financial statements.
    C. consolidated on Confabulated's financial statements only if it is a QSPE.

The following information relates to Problems 19 through 24.

BetterCare Hospitals, Inc. operates a chain of hospitals throughout the United States. The company has been expanding by acquiring local hospitals. Its largest acquisition, that of Statewide Medical, was made under the pooling of interests method. BetterCare complies with U.S. GAAP.

BetterCare is currently forming a 50/50 joint venture with Supreme Healthcare, under which the companies will share control of several hospitals. Supreme Healthcare complies with IFRS and will comply with the preferred accounting methods for joint ventures.

Erik Ohalin is an equity analyst who covers both companies. He has estimated the joint venture's financial information for 2009 in order to prepare his estimates of each company's earnings and financial performance. This information is presented in Exhibit 15-6.

EXHIBIT 15-6 Selected Financial Statement Forecasts for Joint Venture ($ millions)

Year ending 31 December	2009
Revenue	$1,430
Operating income	128
Net income	62
Total assets	1,500
Shareholders' equity	740

BetterCare recently announced it had formed a qualifying special purpose entity through which it can sell up to $100 million of its accounts receivable at any given time. Ohalin wants to estimate the impact this will have on BetterCare's consolidated financial statements.

19. Compared to accounting principles currently in use, the pooling method BetterCare used for its Statewide Medical acquisition has *most likely* caused its reported
    A. revenue to be higher.
    B. total equity to be lower.
    C. total assets to be higher.

20. Based on Ohalin's estimates, the amount of joint venture revenue included on BetterCare's consolidated 2009 financial statements should be *closest* to
    A. $0.
    B. $715.
    C. $1,430.

21. Based on Ohalin's estimates, the amount of joint venture operating income included on the consolidated financial statements of each venturer will *most likely* be
    A. higher for BetterCare.
    B. higher for Supreme Healthcare.
    C. the same for both BetterCare and Supreme Healthcare.

22. Based on Ohalin's estimates, the amount of the joint venture's 31 December 2009 total assets that will be included on Supreme Healthcare's consolidated financial statements will be *closest* to
    A. $0.
    B. $750.
    C. $1,500.

23. Based on Ohalin's estimates, the amount of joint venture shareholders' equity at 31 December 2009 included on the consolidated financial statements of each venturer will *most likely* be
    A. higher for BetterCare.
    B. higher for Supreme Healthcare.
    C. the same for both BetterCare and Supreme Healthcare.

24. If BetterCare uses its special purpose entity, its consolidated financial results will most likely show a *higher*
    A. revenue figure for 2009.
    B. cash balance at 31 December 2009.
    C. accounts receivable balance at 31 December 2009.

CHAPTER 16

MULTINATIONAL OPERATIONS

Timothy S. Doupnik

Moore School of Business
University of South Carolina
Columbia, South Carolina

LEARNING OUTCOMES

After completing this chapter, you will be able to do the following:

- Distinguish local currency, functional currency, and the presentation currency.
- Analyze the impact of changes in exchange rates on the translated sales of the subsidiary and parent company.
- Compare and contrast the current rate method and the temporal method, analyze and evaluate the effects of each on the parent company's balance sheet and income statement, and distinguish which method is appropriate in various scenarios.
- Calculate the translation effects, evaluate the translation of a subsidiary's balance sheet and income statement into the parent company's currency, use the current rate method and the temporal method to analyze how the translation of a subsidiary's financial statements will affect the subsidiary's financial ratios, and analyze how using the temporal method versus the current rate method will affect the parent company's financial ratios.
- Illustrate and analyze alternative accounting methods for subsidiaries operating in hyperinflationary economies.

SUMMARY OVERVIEW

The translation of foreign currency amounts is an important accounting issue for companies with multinational operations. Fluctuations in foreign exchange rates cause the functional currency values of foreign currency assets and liabilities resulting from foreign currency transactions as well as from foreign subsidiaries to change over time, giving rise to foreign

105

exchange differences that must be reflected in the financial statements. Determining how to measure these foreign exchange differences and whether to include them in the calculation of net income are the major issues in accounting for multinational operations.

- The local currency is the national currency of the country where an entity is located. The functional currency is the currency of the primary economic environment in which an entity operates. Normally, the local currency is an entity's functional currency. For accounting purposes, any currency other than an entity's functional currency is a foreign currency for that entity. The currency in which financial statement amounts are presented is known as the presentation currency. In most cases, the presentation currency will be the same as the local currency.
- When an export sale (import purchase) on account is denominated in a foreign currency, the sales revenue (inventory) and foreign currency account receivable (account payable) are translated into the seller's (buyer's) functional currency using the exchange rate on the transaction date. Any change in the functional currency value of the foreign currency account receivable (account payable) that occurs from the transaction date to the settlement date is recognized as a foreign currency transaction gain or loss in net income.
- If a balance sheet date falls between the transaction date and the settlement date, the foreign currency account receivable (account payable) is translated at the exchange rate at the balance sheet date. The change in the functional currency value of the foreign currency account receivable (account payable) is recognized as a foreign currency transaction gain or loss in income. Analysts should understand that these gains and losses are unrealized at the time they are recognized, and might or might not be realized when the transactions are settled.
- A foreign currency transaction gain arises when an entity has a foreign currency receivable and the foreign currency strengthens or it has a foreign currency payable and the foreign currency weakens. A foreign currency transaction loss arises when an entity has a foreign currency receivable and the foreign currency weakens or it has a foreign currency payable and the foreign currency strengthens.
- Companies must disclose the net foreign currency gain or loss included in income. They may choose to report foreign currency transaction gains and losses as a component of operating income or as a component of non-operating income. If two companies choose to report foreign currency transaction gains and losses differently, making a direct comparison of operating profit and operating profit margin between the two companies is questionable.
- To prepare consolidated financial statements, foreign currency financial statements of foreign operations must be translated into the parent company's presentation currency. The major conceptual issues related to this translation process are what is the appropriate exchange rate for translating each financial statement item and how should the resulting translation adjustment be reflected in the consolidated financial statements. Two different translation methods are used worldwide.
- Under the current rate method, assets and liabilities are translated at the current exchange rate, equity items are translated at historical exchange rates, and revenues and expenses are translated at the exchange rate that existed when the underlying transaction occurred. For practical reasons, an average exchange rate is often used to translate income items.
- Under the temporal method, monetary assets (and nonmonetary assets measured at current value) and monetary liabilities (and nonmonetary liabilities measured at current value) are translated at the current exchange rate. Nonmonetary assets and liabilities not measured at current value and equity items are translated at historical exchange rates. Revenues and expenses, other than those expenses related to nonmonetary assets, are translated at the

exchange rate that existed when the underlying transaction occurred. Expenses related to nonmonetary assets are translated at the exchange rates used for the related assets.

- Under both IFRS and U.S. GAAP, the functional currency of a foreign operation determines the method to be used in translating its foreign currency financial statements into the parent's presentation currency and whether the resulting translation adjustment is recognized in income or as a separate component of equity.

- The foreign currency financial statements of a foreign operation that has a foreign currency as its functional currency are translated using the current rate method and the translation adjustment is accumulated as a separate component of equity. The cumulative translation adjustment related to a specific foreign entity is transferred to net income when that entity is sold or otherwise disposed of. The balance sheet risk exposure associated with the current rate method is equal to the foreign subsidiary's net asset position.

- The foreign currency financial statements of a foreign operation that has the parent's presentation currency as its functional currency are translated using the temporal method and the translation adjustment is included as a gain or loss in income. U.S. GAAP refers to this process as *remeasurement*. The balance sheet exposure associated with the temporal method is equal to the foreign subsidiary's net monetary asset/liability position (adjusted for nonmonetary items measured at current value).

- IFRS and U.S. GAAP differ with respect to the translation of foreign currency financial statements of foreign operations located in a highly inflationary country. Under IFRS, the foreign currency statements are first restated for local inflation and then translated using the current exchange rate. Under U.S. GAAP, the foreign currency financial statements are translated using the temporal method, without any restatement for inflation.

- Application of the different translation methods for a given foreign operation can result in very different amounts reported in the parent's consolidated financial statements.

- Companies must disclose the total amount of translation gain or loss reported in income and the amount of translation adjustment included in a separate component of stockholders' equity. Companies are not required to separately disclose the component of translation gain or loss arising from foreign currency transactions and the component arising from application of the temporal method.

- Disclosures related to translation adjustments reported in equity can be used to include these as gains and losses in determining an adjusted amount of income following a clean-surplus approach to income measurement.

Foreign currency translation rules are well-established in both IFRS and U.S. GAAP. Fortunately, except for the treatment of foreign operations located in highly inflationary countries, there are no major differences between the two sets of standards in this area. The ability to understand the impact of foreign currency translation on the financial results of a company using IFRS should apply equally as well in the analysis of financial statements prepared in accordance with U.S. GAAP.

PROBLEMS

The following information relates to Problems 1 through 6.

Pedro Ruiza is an analyst for a credit rating agency. One of the companies he follows, Eurexim SA, is based in France and complies with International Financial Reporting

Standards (IFRS). Ruiz has learned that Eurexim used €220 million of its own cash and borrowed an equal amount to open a subsidiary in Ukraine. The funds were converted into hryvnia (UAH) on 31 December 2007 at an exchange rate of €1.00 = UAH6.70 and used to purchase UAH1,500 million in fixed assets and UAH300 of inventories.

Ruiz is concerned about the effect that the subsidiary's results might have on Eurexim's consolidated financial statements. He calls Eurexim's Chief Financial Officer, but learns little. Eurexim is not willing to share sales forecasts and has not even made a determination as to the subsidiary's functional currency.

Absent more useful information, Ruiz decides to explore various scenarios to determine the potential impact on Eurexim's consolidated financial statements. Ukraine is not currently in a hyperinflationary environment, but Ruiz is concerned that this situation could change. Ruiz also believes the euro will appreciate against the hryvnia for the foreseeable future.

1. If Ukraine's economy becomes highly inflationary, Eurexim will *most likely* translate inventory by
   A. restating for inflation and using the temporal method.
   B. restating for inflation and using the current rate method.
   C. using the temporal method with no restatement for inflation.

2. Given Ruiza's belief about the direction of exchange rates, Eurexim's gross profit margin would be *highest* if it accounts for the Ukraine subsidiary's inventory using
   A. FIFO and the temporal method.
   B. weighted average cost and the temporal method.
   C. weighted average cost and the current rate method.

3. If the euro is chosen as the Ukraine subsidiary's functional currency, Eurexim will translate its fixed assets using the
   A. average rate for the reporting period.
   B. rate in effect when the assets were purchased.
   C. rate in effect at the end of the reporting period.

4. If the euro is chosen as the Ukraine subsidiary's functional currency, Eurexim will translate its accounts receivable using the
   A. rate in effect at the transaction date.
   B. average rate for the reporting period.
   C. rate in effect at the end of the reporting period.

5. If the hryvnia is chosen as the Ukraine subsidiary's functional currency, Eurexim will translate its inventory using the
   A. average rate for the reporting period.
   B. rate in effect at the end of the reporting period.
   C. rate in effect at the time the inventory was purchased.

6. Based on the information available and Ruiza's expectations regarding exchange rates, if the hryvnia is chosen as the Ukraine subsidiary's functional currency Eurexim will *most likely* report
   A. an addition to the cumulative translation adjustment.
   B. a subtraction from the cumulative translation adjustment.
   C. a translation gain or loss as a component of net income.

The following information relates to Problems 7 through 12.

Consolidated Motors is a U.S.-based corporation that sells mechanical engines and components used by electric utilities. Its Canadian subsidiary, Consol-Can, operates solely in Canada. It was created on 31 December 2006 and Consolidated Motors determined at that time that it should use the U.S. dollar as its functional currency.

Chief Financial Officer Monica Templeton was asked to explain to the Board of Directors how exchange rates affect the financial statements of both Consol-Can and the consolidated financial statements of Consolidated Motors. For the presentation, Templeton collects Consol-Can's balance sheets for the years ended 2006 and 2007 (Exhibit 16-1), as well as relevant exchange rate information (Exhibit 16-2).

Templeton explains that Consol-Can uses the FIFO inventory accounting method, and that purchases of C$300 million and the sell-through of that inventory occurred evenly throughout 2007. Her presentation includes reporting the translated amounts in U.S. currency for each item, as well as associated translation related gains and losses. The Board responds with several questions.

• Would there be a reason to change the functional currency to the Canadian dollar?
• Would there be any translation effects for Consolidated Motors if the functional currency for Consol-Can were changed to the Canadian dollar?

EXHIBIT 16-1   Consol-Can Condensed Balance Sheet, Fiscal Years Ending 31 December (C$ millions)

Account	2007	2006
Cash	135	167
Accounts receivable	98	—
Inventory	77	30
Fixed assets	100	100
Accumulated depreciation	(10)	—
Total assets	400	297
Accounts payable	77	—
Long-term debt	175	175
Common stock	100	100
Retained earnings	48	—
Total liabilities and shareholders' equity	400	275

EXHIBIT 16-2   Exchange Rate Information

	C$/US$
Rate on 31 December 2006	0.86
Average rate in 2007	0.92
Weighted average rate for inventory purchases	0.92
Rate on 31 December 2007	0.95

- Would a change in the functional currency have any impact on financial statement ratios for the parent company?
- What would be the balance sheet exposure to translation effects if the functional currency were changed?

7. After translating Consol-Can's inventory and long-term debt into the parent currency (US$), the amounts reported on Consolidated Motor's financial statements at 31 December 2007 would be *closest* to (in millions)
   A. $71 for inventory and $161 for long-term debt.
   B. $71 for inventory and $166 for long-term debt.
   C. $73 for inventory and $166 for long-term debt.

8. After translating Consol-Can's 31 December 2007 balance sheet into the parent currency, the translated value of retained earnings will be *closest to*
   A. $41 million.
   B. $44 million.
   C. $46 million.

9. In response to the Board's first question, Templeton should reply that such a change would be *most* justified if
   A. the inflation rate in the United States became hyperinflationary.
   B. management wanted to flow more of the gains through net income.
   C. Consol-Can were making autonomous decisions about operations, investing, and financing.

10. In response to the Board's second question, Templeton should note that if the change is made, the consolidated financial statements for Consolidated Motors would begin to recognize
    A. realized gains and losses on monetary assets and liabilities.
    B. realized gains and losses on non-monetary assets and liabilities.
    C. unrealized gains and losses on non-monetary assets and liabilities.

11. In response to the Board's third question, Templeton should note that the change will *most likely* affect
    A. the cash ratio.
    B. fixed asset turnover.
    C. receivables turnover.

12. In response to the Board's fourth question, the balance sheet exposure (in millions) would be *closest* to
    A. −19.
    B. 148.
    C. 400.

The following information relates to Problems 13 through 18.
    Romulus Corp. is a U.S.-based company that prepares its financial statements in accordance with U.S. GAAP. Romulus Corp. has two European subsidiaries: Julius and Augustus. Anthony Marks, CFA, is an analyst trying to forecast Romulus's 2008 results. Marks has

prepared separate forecasts for both Julius and Augustus, as well as for Romulus's other operations (prior to consolidating the results.) He is now considering the impact of currency translation on the results of both the subsidiaries and the parent company's consolidated financials.
His research has provided the following insights:

• The results for Julius will be translated into U.S. dollars using the current rate method.
• The results for Augustus will be translated into U.S. dollars using the temporal method.
• Both Julius and Augustus use the FIFO method to account for inventory.
• Julius had year-end 2007 inventory of €340 million. Marks believes Julius will report
  €2300 in sales and €1400 in cost of sales in 2008.

Marks also forecasts the 2008 year-end balance sheet for Julius (Exhibit 16-3). Data and
forecasts related to euro/dollar exchange rates are presented in Exhibit 16-4.

EXHIBIT 16-3   Forecasted Balance Sheet Data
for Julius, 31 December 2008 (€ millions)

Cash	50
Accounts receivable	100
Inventory	700
Fixed assets	1,450
Total assets	2,300
Liabilities	700
Common stock	1,500
Retained earnings	100
Total liabilities and shareholder equity	2,300

EXHIBIT 16-4   Exchange Rates ($/€)

31 December 2007	1.47
31 December 2008	1.61
2008 average	1.54
Rate when fixed assets were acquired	1.25
Rate when 2007 inventory was acquired	1.39
Rate when 2008 inventory was acquired	1.49

13. Based on the translation method being used for Julius, the subsidiary is *most likely*
    A. a sales outlet for Romulus's products.
    B. a self-contained, independent operating entity.
    C. using the U.S. dollar as its functional currency.

14. To account for its foreign operations, Romulus has *most likely* designated the euro as the functional currency for
    A. Julius only.
    B. Augustus only.
    C. both Julius and Augustus.

15. When Romulus consolidates the results of Julius, any unrealized exchange rate holding gains on monetary assets should be
    A. reported as part of operating income.
    B. reported as a nonoperating item on the income statement.
    C. reported directly to equity as part of the cumulative translation adjustment.

16. When Marks translates his forecasted balance sheet for Julius into U.S. dollars, total assets on 31 December 2008 (dollars in millions) will be *closest* to
    A. $1,429.
    B. $2,392.
    C. $3,703.

17. When Marks converts his forecasted income statement data into U.S. dollars, the 2008 gross profit margin for Julius will be *closest* to
    A. 39.1 percent.
    B. 40.9 percent.
    C. 44.6 percent.

18. Relative to the gross margins the subsidiaries' report in local currency, Romulus's consolidated gross margin *most likely*
    A. will not be distorted by currency translations.
    B. would be distorted if Augustus were using the same translation method as Julius.
    C. will be distorted due to the translation and inventory accounting methods Augustus is using.

The following information relates to Problems 19 through 24.

Redline Products, Inc. is a U.S.-based multinational with subsidiaries around the world. One such subsidiary, Acceletron, operates in Singapore, which has seen mild but not excessive rates of inflation. Acceletron was acquired in 2000 and has never paid a dividend. It records inventory using the FIFO method.

Chief Financial Officer Margot Villiers was asked by Redline's Board of Directors to explain how the functional currency selection and other accounting choices affect Redline's consolidated financial statements. She gathers Acceletron's financial statements denominated in Singapore dollars (SGD) in Exhibit 16-5 and the U.S. dollar/Singapore dollar exchange rates in Exhibit 16-6. She does not intend to identify the functional currency actually in use, but rather to use Acceletron as an example of how the choice of functional currency affects the consolidated statements.

19. Compared to using the Singapore dollar as Acceletron's functional currency for 2007, if the U.S. dollar were the functional currency it is *most likely* that Redline's consolidated
    A. inventories will be higher.
    B. receivable turnover will be lower.
    C. fixed-asset turnover will be higher.

EXHIBIT 16-5   Selected Financial Data for Acceletron,
31 December 2007 (SGD millions)

Cash	SGD	125
Accounts receivable		230
Inventory		500
Fixed assets		1,640
Accumulated depreciation		(205)
Total assets	SGD	2,290
Accounts payable		185
Long-term debt		200
Common stock		620
Retained earnings		1,285
Total liabilities and equity		2,290
Total revenues	SGD	4,800
Net income	SGD	450

EXHIBIT 16-6   Exchange Rates Applicable to Acceletron

Exchange Rate in Effect at Specific Times	USD per SGD
Rate when first 1,000 of fixed assets were acquired	0.568
Rate when remaining 640 of fixed assets were acquired	0.606
Rate when long-term debt was issued	0.588
31 December 2006	0.649
Weighted average rate when inventory was acquired	0.654
Average rate in 2007	0.662
31 December 2007	0.671

20. If the U.S. dollar were chosen as the functional currency for Acceletron in 2007, Redline could reduce its balance sheet exposure to exchange rates by
    A. selling SGD 30 of fixed-assets for cash.
    B. issuing SGD 30 of long-term debt to buy fixed assets.
    C. issuing SGD 30 in short-term debt to purchase marketable securities.

21. Redline's consolidated gross profit margin for 2007 would be *highest* if Acceletron accounted for inventory using
    A. FIFO and its functional currency were the U.S. dollar.
    B. LIFO and its functional currency were the U.S. dollar.
    C. FIFO and its functional currency were the Singapore dollar.

22. If the current rate method is used to translate Acceletron's financial statements into U.S. dollars, Redline's consolidated financial statements will *most likely* include Acceletron's
    A. $3,178 in revenues.
    B. $118 in long-term debt.
    C. negative translation adjustment to shareholder equity.

23. If Acceletron's financial statements are translated into U.S. dollars using the temporal method, Redline's consolidated financial statements will *most likely* include Acceletron's
    A. $336 in inventory.
    B. $956 in fixed assets.
    C. $152 in accounts receivable.

24. When translating Acceletron's financial statements into U.S. dollars, Redline is *least likely* to use an exchange rate of USD per SGD
    A. 0.671.
    B. 0.588.
    C. 0.654.

CHAPTER 17

EVALUATING FINANCIAL REPORTING QUALITY

Scott Richardson

Barclays Global Investors
San Francisco, California

İrem Tuna

The Wharton School
University Of Pennsylvania
Philadelphia, Pennsylvania

LEARNING OUTCOMES

After completing this chapter, you will be able to do the following:

- Contrast accrual accounting and cash accounting and explain why accounting discretion exists in an accrual accounting system.
- Describe the relationship between the level of accruals and the persistence of earnings, and the relative multiples which the cash and accrual components of earnings should rationally receive in valuation.
- List and explain the opportunities and motivations for management to intervene in the external financial reporting process, and the mechanisms that discipline such intervention.
- Discuss earnings quality, explain simple measures of earnings quality, and compare and contrast the earnings quality of peer companies.
- Explain mean reversion in earnings and the expected relations between the speed of mean reversion and the accruals component of earnings.
- Identify and explain problems in financial reporting related to revenue recognition, expense recognition, the reporting of assets and liabilities, and the cash flow statement.

- Explain and interpret warning signs of potential problems in each of the major areas of financial reporting (i.e., revenue, expenses, assets, liabilities, and cash flow) and warning signs of overall vulnerability to financial reporting problems.

SUMMARY OVERVIEW

We have touched on major themes in financial reporting quality. This is a broad area with considerable academic and practitioner research. Indeed, many of the techniques described here are used by analysts to make security recommendations and by asset managers in making portfolio allocation decisions. The interested reader would be well served by exploring this topic in greater detail. Among the points the chapter has made are the following:

- Financial reporting quality relates to the accuracy with which a company's reported financial statements reflect its operating performance and to their usefulness for forecasting future cash flows. Understanding the properties of accruals is critical for understanding and evaluating financial reporting quality.
- The application of accrual accounting makes necessary use of judgment and discretion. On average, accrual accounting provides a superior picture to a cash basis accounting for forecasting future cash flows.
- Earnings can be decomposed into cash and accrual components. The accrual component has been found to have less persistence than the cash component, and therefore (1) earnings with higher accrual components are less persistent than earnings with smaller accrual components, all else equal; and (2) the cash component of earnings should receive a higher weighting in evaluating company performance.
- Aggregate accruals = Accrual earnings − Cash earnings.
- Defining net operating assets as $NOA_t = [(\text{Total assets}_t - \text{Cash}_t) - (\text{Total liabilities}_t - \text{Total debt}_t)]$ one can derive the following balance-sheet-based and cash-flow-statement-based measures of aggregate accruals/the accruals component of earnings:

  ○ Aggregate accruals$_t^{B/S}$ = $NOA_t - NOA_{t-1}$

  ○ Aggregate accruals$_t^{CF}$ = $NI_t - (CFO_t + CFI_t)$

  With corresponding scaled measures that can be used as simple measures of financial reporting quality:

  ○ Accruals Ratio$_t^{B/S}$ = $\dfrac{(NOA_t - NOA_{t-1})}{(NOA_t + NOA_{t-1})/2}$

  ○ Accruals ratio$_t^{CF}$ = $\dfrac{[NI_t - (CFO_t + CFI_t)]}{(NOA_t + NOA_{t-1})/2}$

- Aggregate accruals ratios are useful to rank companies for the purpose of evaluating earnings quality. Companies with high (low) accruals ratios are companies with low (high) earnings quality. Companies with low (high) earnings quality tend to experience lower (higher) accounting rates of return and relatively lower excess stock returns in future periods.
- Sources of accounting discretion include choices related to revenue recognition, depreciation choices, inventory choices, choices related to goodwill and other noncurrent assets, choices related to taxes, pension choices, financial asset/liability valuation, and stock option expense estimates.

- A framework for detecting financial reporting problems includes examining reported financials for revenue recognition issues and expense recognition issues.
- Revenue recognition issues include overstatement of revenue, acceleration of revenue, and
  classification of nonrecurring or nonoperating items as operating revenue.
- Expense recognition issues include understating expenses, deferring expenses, and the classification of ordinary expenses as nonrecurring or nonoperating expenses.
- Discretion related to off-balance sheet liabilities (e.g., in the accounting for leases) and the
  impairment of goodwill also can affect financial reporting quality.

PROBLEMS

1. Which of the following mechanisms is *least likely* to discourage management manipula-
   tion of earnings?
   A. Debt covenants.
   B. Securities regulators.
   C. Class action lawsuits.

2. High earnings quality is *most likely* to
   A. Result in steady earnings growth.
   B. Improve the ability to predict future earnings.
   C. Be based on conservative accounting choices.

3. The *best* justification for using accrual-based accounting is that it
   A. Reflects the company's underlying cash flows.
   B. Reflects the economic nature of a company's transactions.
   C. Limits management's discretion in reporting financial results.

4. The *best* justification for using cash-based accounting is that it
   A. Is more conservative.
   B. Limits management's discretion in reporting financial results.
   C. Matches the timing of revenue recognition with that of associated expenses.

5. Which of the following is *not* a measure of aggregate accruals?
   A. The change in net operating assets.
   B. The difference between operating income and net operating assets.
   C. The difference between net income and operating and investing cash flows.

6. Consider the following balance sheet information for Profile, Inc.:

Year ended 31 December	2007	2006
Cash and short-term investments	14,000	13,200
Total current assets	21,000	20,500
Total assets	97,250	88,000
Current liabilities	31,000	29,000
Total debt	50,000	45,000
Total liabilities	87,000	79,000

Profile's balance-sheet-based accruals ratio in 2007 was *closest* to
A. 12.5%.
B. 13.0%.
C. 16.2%.

7. Rodrigue SA reported the following financial statement data for the year ended 2007:

Average net operating assets	39,000
Net income	14,000
Cash flow from operating activity	17,300
Cash flow from investing activity	(12,400)

Rodrigue's cash-flow-based accruals ratio in 2007 was *closest* to
A. −8.5%.
B. −19.1%.
C. 23.3%.

8. Cash collected from customers is *least likely* to differ from sales due to changes in
A. Inventory.
B. Deferred revenue.
C. Accounts receivable.

9. Reported revenue is *most likely* to have been reduced by management's discretionary estimate of
A. Warranty provisions.
B. Inventory damage and theft.
C. Interest to be earned on credit sales.

10. Zimt AG reports 2007 revenue of €14.3 billion. During 2007, its accounts receivable rose by €0.7 billion, accounts payable increased by €1.1 billion, and unearned revenue increased by €0.5 billion. Its cash collections from customers in 2007 were *closest* to
A. €14.1 billion.
B. €14.5 billion.
C. €15.2 billion.

11. Cinnamon Corp. began the year with $12 million in accounts receivable and $31 million in deferred revenue. It ended the year with $15 million in accounts receivable and $27 million in deferred revenue. Based on this information, the accrual-basis earnings included in total revenue were *closest* to
A. $1 million.
B. $7 million.
C. $12 million.

12. Which of the following is *least likely* to be a warning sign of low-quality revenue?
A. A large decrease in deferred revenue.
B. A large increase in accounts receivable.
C. A large increase in the allowance for doubtful accounts.

13. An unexpectedly large reduction in the unearned revenue account is *most likely* a sign that the company

   A. Accelerated revenue recognition.

   B. Overstated revenue in prior periods.

   C. Adopted more conservative revenue recognition practices.

14. Canelle SA reported 2007 revenue of €137 million. Its accounts receivable balance began the year at €11 million and ended the year at €16 million. At year-end, €2 million of receivables had been securitized. Canelle's cash collections from customers (in € millions) in 2007 were *closest* to

   A. €130.

   B. €132.

   C. €134.

15. In order to identify possible understatement of expenses with regard to noncurrent assets, an analyst would *most likely* beware management's discretion to

   A. Accelerate depreciation.

   B. Increase the residual value.

   C. Reduce the expected useful life.

16. A sudden rise in inventory balances is *least likely* to be a warning sign of

   A. Understated expenses.

   B. Accelerated revenue recognition.

   C. Inefficient working capital management.

17. A warning sign that a company may be deferring expenses is sales revenue growing at a slower rate than

   A. Unearned revenue.

   B. Noncurrent liabilities.

   C. Property, plant, and equipment.

18. An asset write-down is *least likely* to indicate understatement of expenses in

   A. Prior years.

   B. Future years.

   C. The current year.

19. Ranieri Corp. reported the following 2007 income statement:

Sales	93,000
Cost of sales	24,500
SG & A	32,400
Interest expense	800
Other income	1,400
Income taxes	14,680
Net income	22,020

Ranieri's core operating margin in 2007 was *closest* to

   A. 23.7%.

   B. 38.8%.

   C. 73.7%.

20. Sebastiani AG reported the following financial results for the years ended 31 December:

	2007	2006
Sales	46,574	42,340
Cost of sales	14,000	13,000
SGA	13,720	12,200
Operating income	18,854	17,140
Income taxes	6,410	5,656
Net income	12,444	11,484

Compared to core operating margin in 2006, Sebastiani's core operating margin in 2007 was
A. Lower.
B. Higher.
C. Unchanged.

21. A warning sign that ordinary expenses are being classified as nonrecurring or nonoperating expenses is
A. Falling core operating margin followed by a spike in positive special items.
B. A spike in negative special items followed by falling core operating margin.
C. Falling core operating margin followed by a spike in negative special items.

22. Which of the following obligations must be reported on a company's balance sheet?
A. Capital leases.
B. Operating leases.
C. Purchase commitments.

23. The *most accurate* estimate for off-balance-sheet financing related to operating leases consists of the sum of
A. future payments.
B. future payments less a discount to reflect the related interest component.
C. future payments plus a premium to reflect the related interest component.

24. The intangible asset goodwill represents the value of an acquired company that cannot be attached to other tangible assets. This noncurrent asset account is charged to an expense
A. As amortization.
B. When it becomes impaired.
C. At the time of the acquisition.

25. Total accruals measured using the balance sheet is *most likely* to differ from total accruals measured using the statement of cash flows when the company has made acquisitions
A. Financed by debt.
B. In exchange for cash.
C. In exchange for stock.

PART II

SOLUTIONS

CHAPTER 1

FINANCIAL STATEMENT ANALYSIS: AN INTRODUCTION

SOLUTIONS

1. B is correct.
   This is the role of financial reporting. The role of financial statement analysis is to evaluate the financial reports.

2. A is correct.
   The balance sheet portrays the current financial position. The income statement and cash flow statement present different aspects of performance.

3. B is correct.
   Profitability is the performance aspect measured by the income statement. The balance sheet portrays the current financial position. The cash flow statement presents a different aspect of performance.

4. A is correct.
   The footnotes disclose choices in accounting methods, estimates, and assumptions.

5. C is correct.
   Although some aspects of management compensation would be found in the footnotes, this is a required disclosure in the proxy statement.

6. C is correct.
   This is a component of management's discussion and analysis.

7. C is correct.
   An unqualified opinion is a "clean" opinion and indicates that the financial statements present the company's performance and financial position fairly.

8. C is correct.
   Ratios are an output of the process data step but are an input into the analyze/interpret data step.

CHAPTER 2

FINANCIAL REPORTING MECHANICS

SOLUTIONS

1. C is correct.

   Sales of products, a primary business activity, are classified as an operating activity. Issuance of debt would be a financing activity. Acquisition of a competitor would be classified as investing activities.

2. A is correct.

   Issuance of debt would be classified as a financing activity. B is incorrect because payment of income taxes would be classified as an operating activity. C is incorrect because investments in common stock would be generally classified as investing activities.

3. A is correct.

   An asset is an economic resource of an entity that will either be converted into cash or consumed.

4. C is correct.

   Owners' equity is a residual claim on the resources of a business.

5. A is correct.

   Assets must equal liabilities plus owners' equity and, therefore, €2,000 = €1,200 + Owners' equity. Owners' equity must be €800.

6. B is correct.

Beginning retained earnings	$1,400
+ Net income	200
− Distributions to owners	(100)
= Ending retained earnings	$1,500

7. C is correct.

Assets = Liabilities + Contributed capital + Beginning retained earnings − Distributions to owners + Revenues − Expenses

Liabilities	$1,000
+ Contributed capital	500
+ Beginning retained earnings	600
− Distributions to owners	(0)
+ Revenues	5,000
− Expenses	(4,300)
= Assets	$2,800

8. C is correct.

This is a contribution of capital by the owners. Assets would increase by $500,000 and contributed capital would increase by $500,000, maintaining the balance of the accounting equation.

9. A is correct.

The payment of January rent represents prepaid rent (an asset), which will be adjusted at the end of January to record rent expense. Cash (an asset) decreases by $12,000. Deposits (an asset) increase by $4,000. Prepaid rent (an asset) increases by $8,000. There is no net change in assets.

10. B is correct.

The sale of products without receipt of cash results in an increase in accounts receivable (an asset) of €10,000. The balance in inventory (an asset) decreases by €8,000. The net increase in assets is €2,000. This would be balanced by an increase in revenue of €10,000 and an increase in expenses (costs of goods sold) of €8,000.

11. C is correct.

The receipt of cash in advance of delivering goods or services results in unearned revenue, which is a liability. The company has an obligation to deliver $30,000 in goods in the future. This balances the increase in cash (an asset) of $30,000.

12. B is correct.

Depreciation is an expense and increases accumulated depreciation. Accumulated depreciation is a contra account which reduces property, plant, and equipment (an asset) by €250,000. Assets decrease by €250,000, and expenses increase by €250,000.

13. A is correct.

The balance sheet shows the financial position of a company at a particular point in time. The balance sheet is also known as a "statement of financial position."

14. B is correct.

The three sections of the statement of cash flows are operating, investing, and financing activities.

15. C is correct.

    Cash received prior to revenue recognition increases cash and deferred or unearned revenue. This is a liability until the company provides the promised goods or services.

16. A is correct.

    When cash is to be received after revenue has been recognized but no billing has actually occurred, an unbilled (accrued) revenue is recorded. Such accruals would usually occur when an accounting period ends prior to a company billing its customer. This type of accrual can be contrasted with a simple credit sale, which is reflected as an increase in revenue and an increase in accounts receivable. No accrual is necessary.

17. B is correct.

    Payment of expenses in advance is called a prepaid expense, which is classified as an asset.

18. C is correct.

    When an expense is incurred and no cash has been paid, expenses are increased and a liability ("accrued expense") is established for the same amount.

19. B is correct.

    The general ledger is the collection of all business transactions sorted by account in an accounting system. The general journal is the collection of all business activities sorted by date.

20. C is correct.

    In order to balance the accounting equation, the company would either need to increase assets or decrease liabilities. Creating a fictitious asset would be one way of attempting to cover up the fraud.

CHAPTER 3

FINANCIAL REPORTING STANDARDS

SOLUTIONS

1. C is correct.
   Providing information about users is not an objective of financial statements. The objectives are to provide information about the entity's financial position, performance, and changes in financial position.

2. B is correct.
   The IASB is currently charged with developing International Accounting Standards. The IASC was the predecessor organization to the IASB.

3. C is correct.
   U.S. Financial Accounting Standards are developed by the FASB.

4. C is correct.
   The SEC requires that shareholders of a company receive a proxy statement prior to a shareholder meeting. Such meetings are held at least once a year, but any special meetings would also require a proxy.

5. C is correct.
   The qualitative characteristics of financial statements according to the IFRS Framework are understandability, relevance, reliability, and comparability.

6. B is correct.
   The Framework recognizes the following constraints on providing relevant, reliable information: timeliness, benefit versus cost, and balancing of the qualitative characteristics.

7. C is correct.
   The IFRS Framework identifies two important underlying assumptions of financial statements: accrual basis and going concern. Going concern is the assumption that the entity will continue to operate for the foreseeable future. Enterprises with the intent to liquidate or materially curtail operations would require different information for a fair presentation.

8. A is correct.
   The IFRS Framework identifies two important underlying assumptions of financial statements: accrual basis and going concern. Accrual basis reflects the effects of transactions and other events being recognized when they occur, not necessarily when cash movements occur. These effects are recorded and reported in the financial statements of the periods to which they relate.

9. B is correct.
   The qualitative characteristic of reliability is contributed to by faithful representation, substance over form, neutrality, prudence, and completeness.

10. C is correct.
    Fair presentation involves both full disclosure and transparency.

11. C is correct.
    Historical cost is the consideration paid to acquire an asset.

12. C is correct.
    The amount that would be received in an orderly disposal is realizable value.

13. C is correct.
    Under IAS No. 1, a complete set of financial statements includes a balance sheet, an income statement, a statement of changes in equity, a cash flow statement, and notes comprising a summary of significant accounting policies and other explanatory notes.

14. B is correct.
    The elements of financial statements related to the measure of performance are income and expenses.

15. A is correct.
    The elements of financial statements related to the measurement of financial position are assets, liabilities, and equity.

16. A is correct.
    Timeliness is not a characteristic of a coherent financial reporting framework. Consistency, transparency, and comprehensiveness are characteristics of a coherent financial reporting framework.

17. A is correct.
    The FASB has been criticized in the past as having a rules-based approach; however, it has indicated that it is moving toward an objectives-oriented approach.

18. B is correct.
    A discussion of the impact would be the most meaningful, although A and C would also be useful.

CHAPTER 4

UNDERSTANDING THE INCOME STATEMENT

SOLUTIONS

1. C is correct.
   IAS No. 1 states that expenses may be categorized by either nature or function.

2. C is correct.
   Cost of goods sold is a classification by function. The other two expenses represent classifications by nature.

3. C is correct.
   Gross profit is revenue minus cost of goods sold. A represents net income and B represents operating income.

4. C is correct.
   Under IFRS, income includes increases in economic benefits from increases in assets, enhancement of assets, and decreases in liabilities.

5. C is correct.
   Net revenue is revenue for goods sold during the period less any returns and allowances, or $1,000,000 − $100,000 = $900,000. A is incorrect; this represents gross profit. B is incorrect; this is the cash collected that is not used under the accrual basis.

6. C is correct.
   The preferred method is the percentage-of-completion method. The completed contract method should be used only when the outcome cannot be measured reliably.

7. A is correct.
   Under the completed contract method, no revenue would be reported until the project is completed. B is incorrect. This is the profit under the percentage-of-completion method. C is incorrect. This is the revenue under the percentage-of-completion method.

8. B is correct.
The installment method apportions the cash receipt between cost recovered and profit using the ratio of profit to sales value (i.e., $3,000,000 \div \$5,000,000 = 60$ percent). Argo will, therefore, recognize $600,000 in profit for 2006 ($1,000,000 cash received $\times$ 60 percent). A uses the cost recovery method and C is the cash received.

9. A is correct.
Under the cost recovery method, the company would not recognize any profit until the cash amounts paid by the buyer exceeded Argo's cost of $2,000,000.

10. C is correct.
Revenue for barter transactions should be measured based on the fair value of revenue from similar nonbarter transactions with unrelated parties.

11. A is correct.
Apex is not the owner of the goods and should only report its net commission as revenue. C is the amount paid to the owners. B is the total amount collected on behalf of the owners.

12. C is correct.
Under the FIFO method, the first 10,000 units sold came from the October purchases at $10, and the next 2,000 units sold came from the November purchases at $11. A is incorrect; this is cost of goods sold under the LIFO method. B is incorrect because it places a cost of $10 on all units.

13. C is correct. Under the weighted average cost method:

October purchases	10,000 units	£100,000
November purchases	5,000 units	£55,000
Total	15,000 units	£155,000

£155,000 $\div$ 15,000 units = £10.3333 $\times$ 12,000 units = £124,000.

14. B is correct.
The LIFO method is not permitted under IFRS. The other methods are permitted.

15. B is correct.
Straight-line depreciation would be ($600,000 − $50,000) $\div$ 10, or $55,000. A assumes the machine was totally expensed in 2007. C ignores the $50,000 residual value.

16. C is correct. Double-declining balance depreciation would be $600,000 $\times$ 20 percent (twice the straight-line rate). A uses 10 percent instead of 20 percent. B applies the depreciation percentage after the residual value has been subtracted from the initial book value.

17. C is correct.
This would result in the highest amount of depreciation in the first year and hence the lowest amount of net income relative to the other choices.

18. A is correct.

    A fire may be infrequent, but it would still be part of continuing operations. IFRS does not permit classification of an item as extraordinary. Discontinued operations relate to a decision to dispose of an operating division.

19. C is correct.

    The weighted average number of shares outstanding for 2007 is 1,050,000. Basic earnings per share would be $1,000,000 \div 1,050,000$, or $0.95. A subtracts the common dividends from net income and uses 1,100,000 shares. B uses the proper net income but 1,100,000 shares.

20. B is correct.

    With stock options, the treasury stock method must be used. Under that method, the company would receive $100,000 (10,000 $\times$ $10) and would repurchase 6,667 shares ($100,000 \div$ $15). The shares for the denominator would be:

Shares outstanding	1,000,000
Options exercises	10,000
Treasury shares purchased	(6,667)
Denominator	1,003,333

CHAPTER 5

UNDERSTANDING THE BALANCE SHEET

SOLUTIONS

1. B is correct.
   Assets are resources controlled by a company as a result of past events.

2. A is correct.
   Assets = Liabilities + Equity and, therefore, Assets − Liabilities = Equity.

3. C is correct.
   A classified balance sheet is one that classifies assets and liabilities as current or noncurrent and provides a subtotal for current assets and current liabilities.

4. B is correct.
   Goodwill is a long-term asset, and the others are all current assets.

5. A is correct.
   Current liabilities are those liabilities, including debt, due within one year. Long-term liabilities are not due within the current year.

6. B is correct.
   The cash received from customers represents an asset. The obligation to provide a product in the future is a liability called "unearned income" or "unearned revenue." Once the product is delivered, the liability will be converted into revenue.

7. C is correct.
   Inventories are carried at historical cost, unless the current replacement cost of the inventory is less.

8. C is correct.
   Paying rent in advance will reduce cash and increase prepaid expenses, both of which are assets.

9. C is correct.
    Accrued liabilities are expenses that have been reported on a company's income statement but have not yet been paid.

10. B is correct.
    Initially, goodwill is measured as the difference between the purchase price paid for an acquisition and the fair value of the acquired company's net assets.

11. C is correct.
    Impairment write-downs reduce equity in the denominator of the debt-to-equity ratio but do not affect debt, so the debt-to-equity ratio is expected to increase. Impairment write-downs reduce total assets but do not affect revenue. Thus, total asset turnover is expected to increase.

12. C is correct.
    For financial assets classified as trading securities, unrealized gains and losses are reported on the income statement and flow to shareholders' equity as part of retained earnings.

13. C is correct.
    For financial assets classified as available for sale, unrealized gains and losses are not recorded on the income statement but do appear on the balance sheet. Shareholders' equity is adjusted through a separate line item for valuation gains and losses termed *other comprehensive income.*

14. A is correct.
    When financial assets are classified as held to maturity, gains and losses are recognized only when realized.

15. B is correct.
    IFRS requires that minority interest in consolidated subsidiaries be classified as shareholders' equity.

16. C is correct.
    Retained earnings are a component of owners' equity.

17. B is correct.
    Share repurchases reduce the company's cash (an asset). Shareholders' equity is reduced because there are fewer shares outstanding and treasury stock is an offset to owners' equity.

18. C is correct.
    Common-size analysis (as presented in the chapter) tells investors how the composition of assets is changing over time. As a result, it can signal when the company is becoming more leveraged.

19. A is correct.
    The current ratio compares assets that can quickly be turned into cash to liabilities that need to be paid within one year. The other ratios are more suited to longer-term concerns.

20. A is correct.

    The cash ratio determines how much of a company's near-term obligations can be settled with existing cash balances.

21. C is correct.

    The debt-to-equity ratio tells how much financial risk a company is exposed to.

22. B is correct.

    The quick ratio ([Cash + Marketable securities + Receivables] ÷ Current liabilities) is 0.81 ([¥779,103 + ¥1,492 + ¥460,202 + ¥1,113,071 − ¥87,709] ÷ ¥2,809,368).

23. C is correct.

    Deferred insurance acquisition costs increased as a percentage of total assets from 3.84 percent in 2004 (¥349,194 ÷ ¥9,090,662) to 3.95 percent in 2005 (¥374,805 ÷ ¥9,499,100). Although the accounts given in choices A and B increased in absolute Japanese yen terms during 2005, these accounts declined as a percentage of total assets in 2005.

24. C is correct.

    The financial leverage ratio (Total assets ÷ Total equity) is 3.31 (¥9,499,100 ÷ ¥2,870,338).

UNDERSTANDING THE CASH FLOW STATEMENT

SOLUTIONS

1. C is correct.

   Answers A and B are incorrect: These are items of information involved in making calculations for the statement of cash flows.

2. B is correct.

   Purchases and sales of long-term assets are considered investing activities. *Note:* Absent information to the contrary, it is assumed that the sale of a building involves cash. If, for example, the transaction had involved the exchange of a building for common stock or the exchange of a building for a long-term note payable, it would have been considered a significant noncash activity.

3. A is correct.

   Answers B and C are items that are included in operating cash flows. *Note*: International accounting standards allow companies to include receipt of interest and dividends as either operating or investing cash flows, and international accounting standards allow companies to include payment of interest and dividends as either operating or financing cash flows.

4. B is correct.

   Noncash transactions, if significant, are reported as supplementary information, not in the investing or financing sections of the cash flow statement.

5. C is correct.

   Interest expense is always classified as an operating cash flow under U.S. GAAP but may be classified as either an operating or financing cash flow under IFRS.

6. A is correct.

   Taxes are required to be separately disclosed on the cash flow statement under IFRS only.

7. A is correct.
The operating section may be prepared under the indirect method. The other sections are always prepared under the direct method.

8. A is correct.
Under the indirect method, the operating section would begin with net income and adjust it to arrive at operating cash flow. The other items would appear under the direct method as a cash flow statement prepared under U.S. GAAP. Note that cash paid for interest may appear on an indirect cash flow statement under IFRS if classified as a financing activity.

9. B is correct.
Revenues of $100 million minus the increase in accounts receivable of $10 million equal $90 million cash received from customers. The increase in accounts receivable means that the company received less in cash than it reported as revenue.

10. B is correct.
Cost of goods sold of $80 million plus the increase in inventory of $5 million equals purchases from suppliers of $85 million. The increase in accounts payable of $2 million means that the company paid $83 million in cash ($85 million minus $2 million) to its suppliers.

11. C is correct.
Cost of goods sold of $75 million less the decrease in inventory of $6 million equals purchases from suppliers of $69 million. The increase in accounts payable of $2 million means that the company paid $67 million in cash ($69 million minus $2 million).

12. C is correct.
Beginning wages payable of $3 million plus wage expense of $20 million, minus ending wages payable of $1 million equals $22 million. The expense of $20 million plus the $2 million decrease in wages payable equals $22 million.

13. C is correct.
Cash received from customers = Sales + the Decrease in accounts receivable = 254.6 + 4.9 = 259.5. Cash paid to suppliers = Cost of goods sold + the Increase in inventory − Increase in accounts payable = 175.9 + 8.8 − 2.6 = 182.1

14. C is correct.
Interest expense of $19 million less the increase in interest payable of $3 million equals $16 million. Tax expense of $6 million plus the decrease in taxes payable of $4 million equals $10 million.

15. C is correct.
Net income (NI) for 2005 can be computed as the change in retained earnings, $25, plus the dividends paid in 2005, $10. NI can also be calculated from the formula: Beginning retained earnings + NI − Dividends paid = Ending retained earnings. Depreciation of $25 would be added back to net income while the increases in accounts receivable, $5, and in inventory, $3, would be subtracted from net income because they are uses of cash.

The decrease in accounts payable is also a use of cash and, therefore, a subtraction from net income. Thus, cash flow from operations for 2005 is $25 + $10 + $25 − $5 − $3 − $7 = $45 ($ millions).

16. C is correct.

   Selling price (cash inflow) minus book value equals gain or loss on sale; therefore, gain or loss on sale plus book value equals selling price (cash inflow). The amount of loss is given, $2 million. To calculate the book value of the equipment sold, find the historical cost of the equipment and the accumulated depreciation on the equipment:

   • Beginning balance of equipment of $100 million plus equipment purchased of $10 million minus ending balance of equipment of $105 million equals the historical cost of equipment sold, or $5 million.

   • Beginning accumulated depreciation of $40 million plus depreciation expense for the year of $8 million minus ending balance of accumulated depreciation of $46 million equals accumulated depreciation on the equipment sold, or $2 million.

   • Therefore, the book value of the equipment sold was $5 million minus $2 million, or $3 million.

   • Because the loss on the sale of equipment was $2 million, the amount of cash received must have been $1 million.

17. A is correct.

   The increase of $42 million in common stock and additional paid-in capital indicates that the company issued stock during the year. The increase in retained earnings of $15 million indicates that the company paid $10 million in cash dividends during the year, determined as beginning retained earnings of $100 million plus net income of $25 million, minus ending retained earnings of $115, which equals $10 million in cash dividends.

18. A is correct.

   To derive operating cash flow, the company would make the following adjustments to net income: add depreciation (a noncash expense) of $2 million; add the decrease in accounts receivable of $3 million; add the increase in accounts payable of $5 million; and subtract the increase in inventory of $4 million. Total additions would be $10 million and total subtractions would be $4 million for net additions of $6 million.

19. C is correct.

   Before examining individual cash flows, the major sources and uses of cash should be evaluated.

20. C is correct.

   The primary source of cash is operating activities. An examination of the financing section indicates that the company pays dividends. The primary use of cash is investing activities. Interest received for Telefónica is classified as an investing activity.

21. B is correct.

   Dividing each line item on the cash flow statement by net revenue is one of two acceptable approaches for preparing a common-size cash flow statement. The other acceptable approach involves expressing each line item of cash inflow (outflow) as a percentage of total inflows (outflows) of cash. Answer A is a description of the indirect method of determining cash flow from operations. Answer C is incorrect because in describing an alternative way to prepare a common-size cash flow statement, it fails to distinguish between the divisor appropriate for cash outflows and cash inflows.

22. B is correct.
Free cash flow to the firm can be computed as operating cash flows plus after-tax interest expense less capital expenditures.

23. A is correct.
This is the interest coverage ratio using operating cash flow rather than earnings before interest, tax, depreciation, and amortization (EBITDA).

CHAPTER 7

FINANCIAL ANALYSIS TECHNIQUES

SOLUTIONS

1. C is correct.
   Cross-sectional analysis involves the comparison of companies with each other for the same time period. Time-series analysis is the comparison of financial data across different time periods.

2. C is correct.
   Solvency ratios are used to evaluate the ability of a company to meet its long-term obligations.

3. A is correct.
   The current ratio is a liquidity ratio. It compares the net amount of current assets expected to be converted into cash within the year, compared with liabilities falling due in the same period. A current ratio of 1.0 would indicate that the company would have just enough current assets to pay current liabilities.

4. C is correct.
   Solvency ratios measure the ability to cover debt payments. There are two main types of solvency ratios. Debt ratios focus on the balance sheet and measure the amount of capital raised by debt relative to equity. Coverage ratios focus on the income statement and measure the ability of a company to cover its debt payments. The fixed charge coverage ratio is a coverage ratio that relates known fixed obligations to the cash flow generated by the entity.

5. C is correct.
   Chan is very *unlikely* to reach the conclusion given in Statement C because days of sales outstanding increased from 23 days in 2003 to 25 days in 2004 to 28 days in 2005, indicating that the time required to collect receivables has increased over the period, which is a negative factor for Spherion's liquidity. By contrast, days of inventory on hand dropped over the period 2003 to 2005, a positive for liquidity. Thus Statement A is an appropriate conclusion. The company's increase in days payable from 35 days to 40 days

shortened its cash collection cycle, thus contributing to improved liquidity; therefore, Statement B is also an appropriate conclusion.

6. A is correct.
   The company is becoming increasingly less solvent, as evidenced by its debt-to-equity ratio increasing from 0.35 to 0.50 from 2003 to 2005. B is incorrect because it incorrectly interprets the debt-to-equity ratio as a measure of liquidity. C is incorrect because it incorrectly interprets the direction of the trend and misinterprets the ratio as an indicator of liquidity.
   Debt to equity:
   2005: $2,000 \div 4,000 = 0.5000$
   2004: $1,900 \div 4,500 = 0.4222$
   2003: $1,750 \div 5,000 = 0.3500$

7. C is correct.
   The decline in the company's equity indicates that the company may be incurring losses on its operations, paying dividends greater than income, or repurchasing shares. Recall that beginning equity + new shares issuance − shares repurchased + net income − dividends = ending equity. A is incorrect because the book value of a company's equity is not affected by changes in the market value of its common stock. B is incorrect because an increased amount of lending does not necessarily indicate that lenders view a company as increasingly creditworthy. Creditworthiness is not evaluated based on how much a company has increased its debt but rather on its willingness to pay its obligations and its ability to pay. (Its financial strength is indicated by its solvency, liquidity, profitability, efficiency, and other aspects of credit analysis.)

8. C is correct.
   The company's problems with its inventory management system causing duplicate orders would result in a higher amount of inventory than needed and would, therefore, likely result in a decrease in inventory turnover. A is incorrect because a more efficient inventory management system would likely be reflected in the inventory turnover ratio, an indicator of more efficient inventory management. B is incorrect because a write-off of inventory at the beginning of the period would decrease the average inventory for the period (the denominator of the inventory turnover ratio), thus increasing the ratio rather than decreasing it.

9. B is correct.
   A write-off of receivables would decrease the average amount of accounts receivable (the denominator of the receivables turnover ratio), thus increasing this ratio. A is incorrect because weaker credit customers are more likely to make payments more slowly or to pose collection difficulties, which would likely increase the average amount of accounts receivable and thus decrease receivables turnover. C is incorrect because a longer payment period would likely increase the average amount of accounts receivable and thus decrease receivables turnover.

10. C is correct.
    Accounts receivable turnover can be calculated to determine the average DSO. Turnovers are equal to $365 \div 19$ (DSO) = 19.2 for 2005 and $365 \div 15 = 24.3$ in 2004. Sales/

turnovers are equal to accounts receivable balances. For 2005, $300,000,000 \div 19.2 =$ $15,625,000, and for 2006, $390,000,000 \div 24.3 = $16,049,383. The difference is an increase in receivables of $424,383.

A is incorrect because the accounts receivable balance must increase.

B is incorrect because the accounts receivable balance must increase.

11. C is correct.

ROE = Return on assets $\times$ Financial leverage. ROA can be decomposed into the product of net profit margin (net income divided by revenue) and total asset turnover (revenue divided by average total assets). Because ROA has been decreasing over 2003 to 2005 while total asset turnover has been increasing, it must be the case that the net profit margin has been declining. Furthermore, because ROE has increased despite the drop in ROA, financial leverage must have increased. Statement C is the only statement that correctly identifies the trends in net profit margin and financial leverage.

12. C is correct.

The increase in the average tax rate in 2005, as indicated by the decrease in the value of the tax burden (the tax burden equals one minus the average tax rate), offset the improvement in efficiency indicated by higher asset turnover); as a result, ROE remained unchanged at 18.90 percent. Statement A is not correct because the EBIT margin, measuring profitability, was unchanged in 2005; furthermore, no information is given on liquidity. Statement B is not correct because profitability was unchanged in 2005.

13. A is correct.

The difference between the two companies' ROE in 2005 is very small and is mainly the result of Company A's increase in its financial leverage, indicated by the increase in its assets/equity ratio from 2 to 4. B is incorrect because Company A has experienced a significant decline in its operating margin, from 10 percent to 7 percent which, all else equal, would not suggest that it is selling more of products with higher profit margin. C is incorrect because the impact of efficiency on ROE is identical for the two companies, as indicated by both companies' asset turnover ratios of 1.5. Furthermore, if Company A had purchased newer equipment to replace older, depreciated equipment, then the company's asset turnover ratio (computed as sales/assets) would have declined, assuming constant sales.

14. A is correct.

The debt-to-equity ratio has improved from 1999 to 2002 from 410 percent to 88 percent (calculations below). The decrease in total debt implies that debt has been repaid, not borrowed. B is incorrect because the company's solvency has deteriorated from 2002 to 2003, as indicated by the higher debt-to-equity ratio. C is incorrect because lower total debt in 2002 suggests repayment of debt.

	2003	2002	2001	2000	1999
Total debt	698,000	521,330	702,506	741,051	847,160
Stockholders' equity	794,830	842,400	405,378	309,371	206,690
Total debt-to-equity ratio	88%	62%	173%	240%	410%

15. A is correct.

    Company A's current ratio of 4.0x ($40,000 ÷ $10,000 = 4.0) indicates it is more liquid than Company B, whose current ratio is only 1.2x ($60,000 ÷ $50,000 = 1.2). Company B is more solvent, as indicated by its lower debt-to-equity ratio of 30 percent ($150,000 ÷ $500,000 = 0.30) compared with Company A's debt-to-equity ratio of 200 percent ($60,000 ÷ $30,000 = 2.0). The other choices are incorrect either because the current ratio is incorrectly calculated or because the debt-to-equity ratio was incorrectly interpreted.

16. C is correct.

    The company's efficiency deteriorated, as indicated by the decline in its total asset turnover ratio from 1.11 (GBP 4,390 ÷ [(GBP 4,384 + 3,500) ÷ 2 = 1.11] for the year 2000 to 0.87 (GBP 11,366 ÷ [(GBP 12,250 + GBP 13,799) ÷ 2] = 0.87) for the year 2004. The decline in the total asset turnover ratio resulted from an increase in average assets from GBP 3,942 [(GBP 4,384 + 3,500) ÷ 2 = GBP 3,942)] in 2000 to GBP 13,024.5 in 2004, an increase of 330 percent, compared with an increase in turnover (i.e., revenues) from GBP 4,390 in 2000 to GBP 11,366 in 2004, an increase of only 259 percent. A is incorrect because the asset turnover ratio is calculated incorrectly. B is incorrect because the current ratio is not an indicator of efficiency.

17. B is correct.

    Comparing 2004 with 2000, the company's solvency deteriorated, as indicated by a decrease in interest coverage from 10.6 (GBP 844 ÷ GBP 80 = 10.6) in 2000 to 8.4 (GBP 1,579 ÷ GBP 188 = 8.4). A is incorrect because it misinterprets the debt-to-asset ratio. C is incorrect because, in isolation, the amount of profits does not provide enough information to assess solvency.

18. C is correct.

    Comparing 2004 with 2000, the company's liquidity improved, as indicated by an increase in its current ratio from 0.71 ([GBP 316 + GBP 558] ÷ GBP 1,223 = 0.71) in 2000 to 0.75 ([GBP 682 + GBP 1,634] ÷ GBP 3,108 + 0.75) in 2004. Note, however, comparing only current investments with the level of current liabilities shows a decline in liquidity from 0.25 (316 ÷ 1223 = 0.25) in 2000 to 0.22 (GBP 682 ÷ GBP 3,108 = 0.22) in 2004. A is incorrect because the debt-to-assets ratio is not an indicator of liquidity. B is incorrect because interest coverage is not an indicator of liquidity.

19. B is correct.

    Comparing 2004 with 2000, the company's profitability deteriorated, as indicated by a decrease in its net profit margin from 11 percent (484 ÷ 4,390 = 0.11) to 5.7 percent (645 ÷ 11,366 = 0.057). A is incorrect because the debt-to-assets ratio is not an indicator of profitability. C is incorrect because growth in shareholders' equity, in isolation, does not provide enough information to assess profitability.

20. B is correct.

    In general, a creditor would consider a decrease in debt to total assets as positive news. As noted in the chapter, a higher level of debt in a company's capital structure increases the risk of default and will result in higher borrowing costs for the company to compensate lenders for assuming greater credit risk.

21. C is correct.

   Assuming no changes in other variables, an increase in average assets would decrease ROA.

22. A is correct.

   The P/E ratio measures the "multiple" that the stock market places on a company's EPS.

CHAPTER 8

INTERNATIONAL STANDARDS CONVERGENCE

SOLUTIONS

1. A is correct.
   Neutrality is a qualitative characteristic. (Timeliness is a constraint and accrual basis is an assumption.)

2. C is correct.
   Changes in the five basic elements (assets, liabilities, equity, income, and expenses) are portrayed in the cash flow statement and the statement of changes in equity.

3. C is correct.
   For available-for-sale securities, there is an asymmetrical treatment of income and changes in value. Under this classification, unrealized gains and losses can accumulate in equity without affecting the income statement.

4. A is correct.
   Whenever possible, the cost of inventory should be assigned by specific identification of the unit's costs. Two alternative formulas for assigning the cost of inventory are weighted average cost and FIFO.

5. C is correct.
   LIFO is not an acceptable inventory costing method.

6. C is correct.
   Like U.S. GAAP, international standards require inventory to be reported at the lower of cost or net realizable value. However, IFRS permit the reversal of inventory write-downs, but no such provision exists in U.S. GAAP.

7. C is correct.
   Unlike U.S. GAAP, international accounting standards allow revaluations (both increases and decreases) for property, plant, and equipment.

8. C is correct.
   When an investor shares the ownership of an investee, as in a joint venture, control is shared and the investor would account for the investment using a proportionate consolidation method, with the equity method as an alternative.

9. B is correct.
   Under IFRS No. 3, goodwill is capitalized and tested for impairment annually.

10. A is correct.
    A gain is recognized if the amount an acquirer pays to buy another company is less than the fair value of the identifiable net assets acquired. Extraordinary gains are not allowed under IFRS.

11. C is correct.
    If an intangible asset does not have a finite life, it is not amortized. Instead, the asset is tested at least annually for impairment (like goodwill).

12. C is correct.
    Any upward revaluation is reported as part of equity, unless it is reversing a previous revaluation decrease.

13. C is correct.
    When the outcome of a contract cannot be reliably estimated, revenue should be recognized to the extent that it is probable to recover contract costs. This differs from U.S. GAAP, which requires that the completed contract method be used in such cases.

14. C is correct.
    In choosing the appropriate depreciation method, IFRS requires that (1) the depreciable amount is allocated on a systematic basis over the useful life, and (2) the method used must reflect the pattern of expected consumption.

15. B is correct.
    IFRS allows cash flows from interest and dividends to be reported as either operating or investing cash inflows. Under U.S. GAAP, these must be reported as operating cash inflows.

16. C is correct.
    IFRS allows cash payments for interest to be reported as either operating or financing cash outflows. Under U.S. GAAP, these must be reported as operating cash outflows.

17. C is correct.
    IFRS allows cash payments for dividends to be reported as either operating or financing cash outflows. Under U.S. GAAP, these must be reported as financing cash outflows.

18. C is correct.
    If comparing a U.S. company that uses LIFO accounting with an international company for whom this method is not allowable, an analyst will make adjustments. Specifically,

using LIFO reserve note disclosures, the analyst will adjust the U.S. company's profits, ending inventory, and total assets.

19. C is correct.

    If comparing a U.S. company with an IFRS company which has written up the value of its intangible assets, an analyst will eliminate the effect of the write-ups in calculating any affected asset-based ratios, which, in this case, includes the financial leverage multiplier (Total assets ÷ Total common equity).

CHAPTER 9

FINANCIAL STATEMENT ANALYSIS: APPLICATIONS

SOLUTIONS

1. A is correct.

   For a large, diversified company, margin changes in different business segments may offset each other. Furthermore, margins are most likely to be stable in mature industries.

2. C is correct.

   Accounts receivable turnover is equal to $365 \div 19$ (collection period in days) $= 19.2$ for 2003 and needs to equal $365 \div 15 = 24.3$ in 2004 for Galambos to meet its goal. Sales/turnover equals the accounts receivable balance. For 2003, $\$300{,}000{,}000 \div 19.2 = \$15{,}625{,}000$, and for 2004, $\$400{,}000{,}000 \div 24.3 = \$16{,}460{,}905$. The difference of $\$835{,}905$ is the increase in receivables needed for Galambos to achieve its goal.

3. C is correct.

   Credit analysts consider both business risk and financial risk.

4. A is correct.

   Requiring that net income be positive would avoid selecting companies that report positive return on equity because both net income and shareholders' equity are negative.

5. C is correct.

   A lower debt-to-total-assets ratio indicates greater financial strength. Requiring that a company's debt-to-total-assets ratio be below a certain cutoff point would allow the analyst to screen out highly leveraged and, therefore, potentially financially weak companies. Requiring declining sales growth (answer A) or negative income (answer B) would not be appropriate for screening out financially weak companies.

6. C is correct.

   Survivorship bias exists when companies that merge or go bankrupt are dropped from the database and only surviving companies remain. Look-ahead bias involves using updated financial information in backtesting that would not have been available at the time the decision was made. Backtesting involves testing models in prior periods and is not a bias itself.

7. C is correct.
   Financial statements should be adjusted for differences in accounting standards (as well as accounting and operating choices). These adjustments should be made prior to common-size and ratio analysis.

8. C is correct.
   IFRS makes a distinction between unrealized gains and losses on available-for-sale debt securities that arise due to exchange rate movements and requires these changes in value to be recognized in the income statement, whereas U.S. GAAP does not make this distinction.

9. A is correct.
   LIFO is not permitted under international financial reporting standards.

10. C is correct.
    To convert LIFO inventory to FIFO inventory, the entire LIFO reserve must be added back: $600,000 + $70,000 = $670,000.

11. C is correct.
    There were no additions or deletions to the fixed asset account during the year, so depreciation expense is equal to the difference in accumulated depreciation at the beginning of the year and the end of the year, or 0.4 million. Average age is equal to accumulated depreciation/depreciation expense, or $1.6 \div 0.4 = 4$ years. Average depreciable life is equal to ending gross investment/depreciation expense $= 2.8 \div 0.4 = 7$ years.

12. C is correct.
    Tangible book value removes all intangible assets, including goodwill, from the balance sheet.

13. C is correct.
    Operating leases can be used as an off-balance-sheet financing technique because neither the asset nor liability appears on the balance sheet. Inventory and capital leases are reported on the balance sheet.

14. C is correct.
    The present value of future operating lease payments would be added to total assets and total liabilities.

CHAPTER 10

INVENTORIES

SOLUTIONS

1. C is correct.

   Transportation costs incurred to ship inventory to customers is an expense and may not be capitalized in inventory. (Transportation costs incurred to bring inventory to the business location can be capitalized in inventory.) Storage costs required as part of production, as well as costs incurred due to normal waste of materials can be capitalized in inventory. (Costs incurred due to abnormal waste must be expensed.)

2. B is correct.

   Ajax can allocate to inventory cost a portion of fixed production overhead based on normal capacity levels. Normal capacity is 10 million pencils, and fixed production costs are $1 million, so capitalized inventory costs will include 90% (9 million pencils produced ÷ 10 million capacity) of the fixed production overhead costs of $1 million. The inventory cost for each pencil related to the fixed production overhead allocated to each pencil is thus $0.10 (90% × $1 million ÷ 9 million pencils). The remaining $100,000 of fixed production overhead costs would be expensed as incurred.

3. B is correct.

   Inventory expense includes costs of purchase, costs of conversion, and other costs incurred in bringing the inventories to their present location and condition. It does not include storage costs not required as part of production.

4. A is correct.

   IAS 41 allows (and U.S. GAAP treatment is similar) the inventories of producers and dealers of agricultural and forest products, agricultural produce after harvest, and minerals and mineral products to be carried at net realizable value even if above historical cost.

5. A is correct.

   Under U.S. GAAP, inventory is carried at the lower of cost or market value. After being written down a new cost basis is determined and further revisions may only reduce the value further.

6. A is correct.

   IFRS permit the reversal of inventory write-downs, U.S. GAAP does not.

7. B is correct.

   Cinnamon uses the weighted average cost method, so in 2008, 5,000 units of inventory were 2007 units at €10 each and the 50,000 were 2008 purchases at €11. The weighted average cost of inventory during 2008 was thus $(5,000 \times 10) + (50,000 \times 11) = 50,000 + 550,000 = €600,000$ and the weighted average cost was €600,000/55,000 = €10.91. Cost of goods sold were €10.9091 × 45,000, which is approximately €490,909.

8. C is correct.

   Zimt uses the FIFO method, and thus the first 5,000 units sold in 2008 depleted the 2007 inventory. Of the inventory purchased in 2008, 40,000 units were sold and 10,000 remain, valued at €11 each for a total of €110,000.

9. A is correct.

   Zimt uses the FIFO method, so its cost of goods sold represents units purchased at a (no longer available) lower price. Nutmeg uses the LIFO method, so its cost of goods sold is approximately equal to the current replacement cost of inventory.

10. B is correct.

    Nutmeg uses the LIFO method and thus some of the inventory on the balance sheet was purchased at a (no longer available) lower price. Zimt uses the FIFO method, so the carrying value on the balance sheet represents the most recently purchased units and thus approximates the current replacement cost.

11. B is correct.

    In a declining price environment, the newest inventory is the lowest cost inventory. In such circumstances, using the LIFO method (selling the newer, cheaper inventory first) will result in lower cost of goods sold and higher profit.

12. B is correct.

    In a rising price environment, inventory balances will be higher for the company using the FIFO method. Accounts payable are based on amounts due to suppliers, not the amounts accrued based on inventory accounting.

13. C is correct.

    The write-down reduced the value of inventory and increased cost of goods sold in 2007. The higher numerator and lower denominator mean that the inventory turnover ratio as reported was too high. Gross margin and the current ratio were both too low.

14. A is correct.

    The reversal shifted cost of sales from 2008 to 2007. As a result, the reported 2008 profits were overstated. Inventory balance would have been the same because the write-down and reversal cancel each other out. Cash flow from operations is not affected by the non-cash write-down, but the higher profits in 2008 likely resulted in higher taxes and thus lower cash flow from operations.

15. B is correct.

    LIFO will result in lower inventory and higher cost of sales. Gross margin (a profitability ratio) will be lower, the current ratio (a liquidity ratio) will be lower, and inventory turnover (an efficiency ratio) will be higher.

16. A is correct.

    Because inventory purchases exceed product sales there is no LIFO liquidation and thus no abnormal "phantom" profits. Consequently, LIFO results in lower gross margin than FIFO.

17. C is correct.

    Under FIFO, cost of goods sold would be lower than LIFO by an amount equal to the increase in the LIFO reserve (in this case, $63.3 - $56.8 = $6.5). So, $1,827 - $6.5 = $1,820.5 meaning gross profit is $2,157 - $1,820.5 = $336.5.

18. A is correct.

    Inventory turnover is cost of goods sold divided by average inventory. As reported, this was $1,827/$557.5 = 3.28. Under FIFO, cost of goods sold would have been $1,820.5 and inventory would have been $616.3 and $618.8 (average $617.6). Adjusted inventory turnover would thus be 2.96.

19. B is correct.

    The LIFO method increases cost of sales, thus reducing profits and the taxes thereon.

20. A is correct.

    The adjustments are to add the LIFO reserve to inventory and subtract the change in LIFO reserve from cost of goods sold.

21. A is correct.

    U.S. GAAP does not permit inventory write-downs to be reversed.

CHAPTER 11

LONG-LIVED ASSETS

SOLUTIONS

1. C is correct.

   Capitalization of interest costs incurred during construction is permitted under both U.S. GAAP and IFRS.

2. A is correct.

   To adjust solvency ratios, interest capitalized during the period should be *added* to interest expense. Any related depreciation expense would be added to *income*.

3. B is correct.

   By acquiring its drug, Biotech Holdings will have higher total assets (because it would capitalize the intangible asset) and higher cash flow from operations (because the drug purchase would appear as an investing cash flow). All else equal, Biotech Holdings would initially report higher net income because only a portion of the cost would reduce revenues in the current accounting period (through depreciation). In future periods, Advanced Biotech would report higher net income so that total net income over time would be unaffected by whether R&D was expensed or amortized.

4. A is correct.

   Under U.S. GAAP, acquired in-process research and development costs are expensed upon acquisition. In contrast, companies reporting under IFRS may either identify in-process R&D as a separate asset with a finite life, or include it as part of goodwill.

5. C is correct.

   Under IFRS, development-phase R&D may be capitalized, whereas it must be expensed under U.S. GAAP (except for software under certain circumstances). Both standards require *expensing* of research-phase expenditures, and IFRS requires acquired in-process R&D to be capitalized.

6. B is correct.

   All else equal, net income would be more volatile if AIC expensed the cost of the machine because the entire cost would detract from net income in the year of its purchase.

7. A is correct.
   Over the life of the asset, depreciation expense will be $900,000 regardless of the depreciation method chosen.

8. A is correct.
   Expensing results in the lower ROE in the first year, but a higher ROE in subsequent years.

9. B is correct.
   Depreciation expense will be lower if the straight-line method is used. That will increase reported income and therefore reported income taxes. Although the company will use MACRS for tax purposes, the difference will be in deferred taxes on the balance sheet until reversed.

10. B is correct.
    The average remaining life is calculated as net PP&E divided by annual depreciation expense. Net PP&E is $15,104 ($22,983 − $7,879). Annual depreciation expense is $2,459, giving an average remaining life of 6.14 years ($15,104 ÷ $2,459).

11. A is correct.
    Average age is calculated as accumulated depreciation divided by annual depreciation expense. It is 11.5, 17.4, and 14.4 for airlines A, B and C, respectively.

12. C is correct.
    Assets with indefinite lives are not amortized. Therefore, no deduction is taken from the asset over time or charged to the income statement. Assets and net income are both higher.

13. B is correct.
    Amortization expense is determined by dividing the difference between the acquisition and salvage values over the useful life. Higher salvage values and longer lives equate to lower amortization expense and thus higher profit margins.

14. A is correct.
    Higher amortization expense reduces reported income and the taxes paid on the income. On the cash flow statement, the amortization is added back as a noncash expense. Therefore, the cash flow will be highest when amortization is highest because the amortization is added back, but the tax outflow is reduced. Amortization is highest for shorter useful lives and lower salvage value estimates.

15. B is correct.
    At the time the expense is estimable the company must create a new liability equal to the discounted value of the future cash outlay. The liability will increase in size over time as the maturity approaches (the discount is reduced). Only at the time of disposal will the liability be reduced (removed). When first established the liability is offset by increasing the carrying value of the asset. Over time, the asset value is reduced by charging it to expense.

16. B is correct.

    AROs do not result in one-time charges but in a liability that increases over time and offset by charges to income. The result is rising liability and lower equity (relative to assets that will not require a retirement obligation) as the retirement date approaches.

17. B is correct.

    A credit analyst would want to treat the ARO as an interest-bearing liability. The necessary adjustments would be to reduce the ARO by the value of any offsetting assets and future tax benefits, to reclassify accretion expense as interest expense, and to increase total debt by the amount of the ARO. No adjustments to shareholders' equity are needed.

18. A is correct.

    Fisherman is depreciating $90,000 annually [($1,000,000 − $100,000) ÷ 10]. After five years the depreciation totals $450,000 and the book value of the asset is $550,000 ($1,000,000 − $450,000). It must record a $50,000 loss on the sale. Material losses are recorded as a separate line item.

19. C is correct.

    At the time an asset is sold, the company records a gain or loss equal to the difference between the sale price and the carrying price. At the time the decision is made, the carrying value is adjusted to the lower of book value or estimated fair value. Either a gain or loss can occur at the time of sale, but only a loss can result at the time the decision is made.

20. B is correct.

    An asset is impaired when its carrying value exceeds its fair value.

21. A is correct.

    Asset impairments do not affect cash flow or current period depreciation. However, by reducing the value of the asset (and thus the difference between book and salvage value) the impairment will affect future depreciation expense.

22. A is correct.

    Neither U.S. GAAP nor IFRS permits goodwill amortization. By contrast, each of the other choices is treated differently depending on which standards are applied.

23. B is correct.

    Upward revaluations increase total assets, shareholders' equity, and depreciation expense. Therefore, profitability ratios (e.g. ROE) would decrease. Reported leverage (average total assets divided by average shareholders' equity) would also decrease.

CHAPTER 12

INCOME TAXES

SOLUTIONS

1. C is correct.

   Because the differences between tax and financial accounting will correct over time, the resulting deferred tax asset, for which the expense was charged to the income statement but the tax authority has not yet been paid, will be a temporary difference. A valuation allowance would only arise if there was doubt over the company's ability to earn sufficient income in the future to require paying the tax.

2. A is correct.

   The taxes a company must pay in the immediate future are taxes payable.

3. B is correct.

   Higher reported tax expense relative to taxes paid will increase the deferred tax asset, whereas lower reported tax expense relative to taxes paid increases the deferred tax liability.

4. B is correct.

   If the liability is expected to reverse (and thus require a cash tax payment), the deferred tax represents a future liability.

5. A is correct.

   If the liability will not reverse, there will be no required tax payment in the future and the "liability" should be treated as equity.

6. C is correct.

   The deferred tax liability should be excluded from both debt and equity when both the amounts and timing of tax payments resulting from the reversals of temporary differences are uncertain.

7. C is correct.

   Accounting items that are not deductible for tax purposes will not be reversed and thus result in permanent differences.

8. C is correct.

   Tax credits that directly reduce taxes are a permanent difference, and permanent differences do not give rise to deferred tax.

9. A is correct.
   The capitalization will result in an asset with a positive tax base and zero carrying value. The amortization means the difference is temporary. Because there is a temporary difference on an asset resulting in a higher tax base than carrying value, a deferred tax asset is created.

10. B is correct.
    The difference is temporary, and the tax base will be lower (because of more rapid amortization) than the carrying value of the asset. The result will be a deferred tax liability.

11. A is correct.
    The advances represent a liability for the company. The carrying value of the liability exceeds the tax base (which is now zero). A deferred tax asset arises when the carrying value of a liability exceeds its tax base.

12. B is correct.
    The income tax provision in 2007 was $54,144, consisting of $58,772 in current income taxes, of which $4,628 was deferred.

13. B is correct.
    The effective tax rate of 30.1 percent ($56,860/$189,167) was higher than the effective rates in 2005 and 2007.

14. A is correct.
    In 2007 the effective tax rate on foreign operations was 24.2 percent [($28,140 + $124) ÷ $116,704] and the effective U.S. tax rate was [($30,632 − $4,752) ÷ $88,157] = 29.4 percent. In 2006 the effective tax rate on foreign operations was 26.2 percent and the U.S. rate was 35.9 percent. In 2005 the foreign rate was 24.1 percent and the U.S. rate was 35.5 percent.

15. B is correct.
    The valuation allowance is taken against deferred tax assets to represent uncertainty that future taxable income will be sufficient to fully utilize the assets. By decreasing the allowance, Zimt is signaling greater likelihood that future earnings will be offset by the deferred tax asset.

16. C is correct.
    The valuation allowance is taken when the company will "more likely than not" fail to earn sufficient income to offset the deferred tax asset. Because the valuation allowance equals the asset, by extension the company expects *no* taxable income prior to the expiration of the deferred tax assets.

17. A is correct.
    A lower tax rate would increase net income on the income statement, and because the company has a net deferred tax liability, the net liability position on the balance sheet would also improve (be smaller).

18. C is correct.

The reduction in the valuation allowance resulted in a corresponding reduction in the income tax provision.

19. B is correct.

The net deferred tax liability was smaller in 2007 than it was in 2006, indicating that in addition to meeting the tax payments provided for in 2007 the company also paid taxes that had been deferred in prior periods.

20. C is correct.

The income tax provision at the statutory rate of 34 percent is a benefit of $112,000, suggesting that the pre-tax income was a loss of $112,000 ÷ 0.34 = ($329,412). The income tax provision was $227,000. ($329,412) − $227,000 = ($556,412).

21. C is correct.

Accounting expenses that are not deductible for tax purposes result in a permanent difference, and thus do not give rise to deferred taxes.

22. B is correct.

Over the three-year period, changes in the valuation allowance reduced cumulative income taxes by $1,670,000. The reductions to the valuation allowance were a result of the company being "more likely than not" to earn sufficient taxable income to offset the deferred tax assets.

CHAPTER 13

LONG-TERM LIABILITIES
AND LEASES

SOLUTIONS

1. B is correct.
   The company receives $1 million in cash from investors at the time the bonds are issued. This is recorded as a financing activity.

2. A is correct.
   At the time of issue, both companies will record a $1 million liability and cash from financing inflow. The income statement will reflect interest expense equal to the cash interest payments PLUS amortization of the initial discount. Because both companies received the same amount, the bonds issued at a discount will have a higher face value and higher periodic interest expense on the income statement. However, the amortization is a noncash expense and will not appear on the statement of cash flows.

3. A is correct.
   In the United States, expenses incurred when issuing bonds are generally recorded as an asset and amortized to the related expense (legal, etc.) over the life of the bonds. The related cash flows are financing and operating activities, not investing activities.

4. B is correct.
   The bonds will be issued at a discount because the market interest rate is higher than the stated rate. Discounting the future payments to their present value indicates that at the time of issue the company will record $978,938 as both a liability and a cash inflow from financing activities. During the year, the company will pay a cash outflow from operating activities of $55,000 related to the interest payment, but interest expense on the income statement will also reflect $3,736 related to amortization of the initial discount, for a total interest expense of $58,736. The value of the liability at 31 December 2008 will reflect the initial value plus the amortized discount, for a total of $982,674.

5. A is correct.
   The stated rate on the bonds is higher than the market rate, which indicates the bonds will be issued at a premium. Taking the present value of each payment indicates an issue date value of $10,210,618. The interest expense is determined by multiplying the

167

book value at the beginning of the period ($10,210,618) by the market interest rate at the time of issue (6.0 percent) for an interest expense of $612,637. The value after one year will equal the beginning value less the amortized premium, which is the difference between the amount paid ($650,000) and the expense accrued ($612,637) or $37,363. $10,210,618 − $37,363 = $10,173,255 or $10.17 million.

6. A is correct.
Both bonds will add $10 million to debt and nothing to equity, and thus have the same effect on the debt/equity ratio at the time they are issued. However, the value of the liability for zero-coupon bonds increases as the discount is amortized over time while the liability will not change for the par bonds. Furthermore, the amortized interest will reduce earnings at an increasing rate over time as the value of the liability increases. Higher relative debt and lower relative equity (through retained earnings) will cause the debt/equity ratio to increase as the zero-coupon bonds approach maturity, compared to the bonds issued at par.

7. A is correct.
When interest rates rise, bonds decline in value. Thus, the book value of the bonds being carried on the balance sheet is higher than the market value. The company could repurchase the bonds for less than book value, so the economic liabilities are overestimated. Because the bonds are fixed rates, there is no effect on interest coverage.

8. C is correct.
Covenants protect debtholders from excessive risk-taking, typically by limiting the issuer's ability to use cash or by limiting the overall levels of debt relative to income and equity. Issuing additional equity would increase the company's ability to meet its obligations, so debtholders would not restrict that ability.

9. B is correct.
Because convertible bonds have characteristics of both debt and equity, at times it can be appropriate to treat it as debt, equity, or both. Because it is already classified as debt, adjusting debt but not adjusting equity would have the effect of ignoring it altogether. Such treatment would be inappropriate.

10. B is correct.
If the bonds are converted, liabilities decrease by the book value of the bonds and equity increases by the same amount.

11. C is correct.
If the current market price is significantly above the conversion price, the bonds are more likely to be converted into equity than redeemed at face value. Therefore, it would be appropriate to treat the bonds as equity.

12. A is correct.
If converted, debt would decrease by $200 million and equity would increase by the same amount. The resulting debt-to-equity ratio would be $200/$500 = 0.40.

13. C is correct.
Assets held under a synthetic lease enjoy the tax benefits of ownership (depreciation expense) but are not held as assets or liabilities on the financial statements.

14. B is correct.

An operating lease is not recorded on the balance sheet (debt is lower), and lease payments are entirely categorized as rent (interest expense is lower.) Because the rent expense is an operating outflow but principal repayments are financing cash flows, the operating lease will result in lower cash flow from operating activity.

15. A is correct.

The finance leases are carried as liabilities in the amount of the present value of future minimum lease payments (equals the sum of future minimum lease payments *minus* the sum of amounts representing interest). Using the alternative short cut approach shown in Example 13-12 (solution to 2), Xu could estimate the present value of the operating lease payments by multiplying the aggregate minimum future operating lease payments ($25 million) by the ratio of the present value of minimum finance lease payments ($20 million − $6 million = $14 million) to the undiscounted minimum finance lease payments ($20 million). The result is: ($14 million ÷ $20 million) × $25 million = $17.5 million.

16. A is correct.

In the early years, a finance lease generally results in higher reported expenses, lower profitability, and a lower ROE. This difference reverses over the life of the lease such that finance leases will result in an ROE that rises over time and ends higher than would result if an operating lease were used.

17. B is correct.

When a lease is classified as an operating lease, the underlying asset remains on the lessor's balance sheet. The lessor will record a depreciation expense that reduces the assets value over time.

18. A is correct.

A sales-type lease treats the lease as a sale of the asset, and revenue is recorded at the time of sale equal to the present value of future lease payments. Under a direct financing lease, only interest income is reported as earned. Under an operating lease, revenue from rent is reported when collected.

19. C is correct.

With an operating lease, all revenue is recorded as rental revenue. A portion of the payments for either direct financing or sales-type leases is reported as interest income.

20. C is correct.

The current debt to total capital ratio is 840 ÷ (840 + 520) = 0.62. To adjust for the purchase commitments, an analyst should add 100 to both the numerator and denominator: 940 ÷ (940 + 520) = 0.64.

21. B is correct.

McKinnon should add $60 million to accounts receivable, reduce cash from operating activities by $50 million, and increase cash from financing activities by $50 million.

CHAPTER 14

EMPLOYEE COMPENSATION: POSTRETIREMENT AND SHARE-BASED

SOLUTIONS

1. B is correct.

   The benefit obligation used to calculate pension liabilities is the PBO.

2. A is correct.

   The economic pension expense is calculated as follows:

Change in benefit obligation	$115
Benefits paid	1,322
Adjusted change in liability	$1,437
Change in plan assets	$673
Employer contributions	−693
Benefits paid	1,322
Adjusted change in assets	$1,302
Economic pension expense	$135
Alternatively:	
Underfunding, beginning of 2008	−$4,984
Underfunding, end of 2008	−4,426
Change in underfunding	$558
Employer contribution	$693
Less change in underfunding	558
Economic pension expense	$135

3. A is correct.
   The economic pension expense is $135 million. Magenta's reported pension expense (net periodic benefit cost) for the period is $43 million. The difference is $135 million − $43 million = $92 million.

4. B is correct.
   The company's economic pension expense is $135 million, but its reported pension expense is $43 million, a difference of $92 million. That amount must be adjusted for taxes: $92 million × (1 − 0.40) = $55.2 million. The economic pension expense is higher than the reported pension expense so net income would be adjusted down by about $55 million.

5. B is correct.
   The balance sheet as reported shows only the net liability of $28,531 million − $24,105 million = $4,426 million. In order to fully reflect the plan's economic position, the gross asset and liability should be reported rather than the net. Doing so requires adding $24,105 million to both assets and liabilities.

6. B is correct.
   Magenta's economic pension expense for the period was $135 million. The company's contributions to the plan for the year were $693 million. The $558 million difference between these numbers can be viewed as a reduction of the overall pension obligation. To adjust the statement of cash flows to reflect this view, an analyst would reclassify the $558 million as an outflow related to financing activities rather than operating activities.

7. A is correct.
   Under U.S. GAAP, Passaic's balance sheet reflects the net funded position of the plan. In this case, fund assets of $46,203 less the ending benefit obligation of $45,582 results in a net asset of $621.

8. B is correct.
   The pension expense recorded on the income statement is the $1,050 net periodic benefit cost.

9. A is correct.
   The company's contributions to pension plans are deducted from net income as part of the reconciliation between net income and cash flow from operating activities. In other words, it is the company's contribution ($526 for 2008) that appears on the statement of cash flows.

10. A is correct.
    In 2008 the service cost was $908. Service costs represent the estimated increase in the pension obligation resulting from employees' service during the period.

11. C is correct.
    In 2007 the plan was underfunded (net liability) by $1,699. In 2008 it was overfunded by $621. Only these net values are reflected as an asset or a liability. The change in

funded position, $621 − (−$1,699) = $2,320, is recorded as a change in other comprehensive income within shareholders' equity.

12. A is correct.
In 2008 Passaic used a lower volatility assumption than it did in 2007. Lower expected volatility reduces the fair value of an option and thus the reported expense. Using the 2007 volatility estimate would have resulted in higher expense and thus lower net income.

13. C is correct.
The assumed long-term rate of return on plan assets is not a component of the pension liability (balance sheet). It is used in calculating pension expense (income statement).

14. B is correct.
A higher discount rate will reduce the present value of the pension obligation. In most cases the lower obligation will have a greater impact on interest cost than the higher discount rate. The cash flow from operating activities should not be affected by the change.

15. B is correct.
In 2008 all three assumptions were lower than in 2007. Reducing expected salary increases reduces the periodic service cost. Reducing the discount rate or expected return on plan assets typically increases pension expense.

16. C is correct.
Although the company's inflation estimates have consistently risen over the three-year period, its expectations for salary increases have fluctuated up and down while its assumed discount rate has steadily fallen. Normally both salary increases and the discount rate will be positively related to inflation. Further, although the allocation to equity securities has increased and the discount rate (which should be similar to the return on fixed income investments) is virtually unchanged from 2007 to 2008, the expected return on plan assets is lower in 2008. The higher equity allocation should permit a higher expected return.

17. B is correct.
A higher volatility assumption increases the value of the stock option and thus the compensation expense, which in turn reduces net income. There is no associated liability for stock options.

18. C is correct.
A higher dividend yield reduces the value of the call option and thus option expense. The lower expense results in higher earnings. Higher discount rates and expected lives result in higher call option values.

19. A is correct.
The accumulated benefit obligation at year-end 2008 is €10,018 and represents the amount employees have earned based on their service up until the time measured, regardless of whether the benefits have vested.

20. C is correct.

To reflect the underlying economic pension expense, Kordt would measure the change in funded status excluding employer contributions and benefits paid. The adjustments would be *adding* €423 to the change in benefit obligation, *adding* €423 to the change in the value of plan assets, and *subtracting* €323 from the value of plan assets.

21. A is correct.

The net periodic cost of €143 is the amount recognized on the income statement.

22. C is correct.

The net funded status of the plan is €1,822, but only €1,155 is recognized on the balance sheet: an asset of €2,097, a liability of €942, and net assets (equity) of €1,155. The net result of balance sheet adjustments would be an increase of €1,822 − €1,155 = €667 to shareholders' equity. In other words, whether or not the full amount of assets and liabilities are included on the balance sheet, the actual funded status shows the underlying financial position, and that is a net asset (equity) of €1,822, or €667 higher than is reported.

23. B is correct.

Using the higher 2006 rate of compensation increase would have increased periodic service cost and the benefit obligation, reducing net income. It would not affect prior service costs and related amortization.

24. C is correct.

Using the lower 2006 expected return on plan assets would increase pension expense, reduce net income, and have no effect on plan assets.

CHAPTER 15

INTERCORPORATE INVESTMENTS

SOLUTIONS

1. B is correct.
   Dividends from equity securities that are classified as available-for-sale are included in income when earned. Cinnamon would record its 19 percent share of the dividends paid by Cambridge, which amounted to $3.8 million. Though the value of Cinnamon's stake in Cambridge Processing rose by $2 million during the year, under U.S. GAAP any unrealized gains or losses for available-for-sale securities are reported in the equity section of the balance sheet as part of other comprehensive income until the securities are sold.

2. C is correct.
   If we knew whether Cinnamon had controlling interest or just significant influence, we could then determine whether the equity method or the purchase method would be more likely. U.S. GAAP does not allow the proportionate consolidation method except in certain cases (and never when the reporting company is incorporated, as is Cinnamon).

3. B is correct.
   Net assets (shareholders' equity) are not affected by the choice of accounting method for active investments in other entities.

4. C is correct.
   If Cinnamon is deemed to have significant influence, it would report under the equity method none of Cambridge's revenue but half of its net income ($20). Its profit margin would then be higher than if it also reported half of Cambridge's revenue (control which implies consolidation method) or if it only reported 19 percent of Cambridge's dividends (no change in ownership).

5. A is correct.
   If control is assumed, Cinnamon would consolidate 100 percent of Cambridge's debt, but under U.S. GAAP it would net out the 50 percent minority interest to arrive at shareholders' equity. It is likely that the debt/equity ratio would be higher if 100 percent of Cambridge's debt but only half of its equity were included on Cinnamon's financial statements.

6. A is correct.

   Cambridge has a lower operating margin (88/1,100 = 8.0%) than Cinnamon (142/1,575 = 9.0%). If Cambridge's results are consolidated with Cinnamon's, the consolidated operating margin will reflect that of the combined company, or 230/2,675 = 8.6%.

7. B is correct.

   Oxbow was classified as a held-for-trading security. Held-for-trading securities are reported at fair value, with unrealized gains and losses included in income. The income statement also includes dividends from equity securities that are classified as held for trading. The €3 million decline in the value of Zimt's stake would reduce income by that amount. However, Zimt would record its share of the dividends paid (0.1 × 20 = 2 million). The net effect of Zimt's stake in Oxbow Limited would be to reduce Zimt's income before taxes by €1 million for 2008.

8. A is correct.

   When a company is deemed to have control of another entity, it records all of the other entity's assets on its own consolidated balance sheet. None of the assets would be recorded under an assumption of significant influence.

9. A is correct.

   If Zimt is deemed to have significant influence, it would use the equity method to record its ownership. Under the equity method, Zimt's share of Oxbow's net income would be recorded on a single line (after operating income.) None of the revenue or operating expenses (which comprise operating income) are reported.

10. B is correct.

    Under the proportionate consolidation method, Zimt's balance sheet would show its own total liabilities of €1,421 − 735 = €686 plus half of Oxbow's liabilities of €1,283 − 706 = €577. €686 + (0.5 × 577) = €974.5.

11. C is correct.

    Under the assumption of control, Zimt would record its own sales plus 100 percent of Oxbow's. €1,700 + 1,350 = €3,050.

12. C is correct.

    Net income is not affected by the accounting method used to account for active investments in other companies.

13. C is correct.

    Trading and available-for-sale securities are carried at market value, whereas held-to-maturity securities are carried at historical cost. €28,000 + 40,000 + 50,000 = €118,000.

14. C is correct.

    If Dumas had been classified as a held-for-trading security, its carrying value would have been the €55,000 fair value rather than the €50,000 historical cost.

15. B is correct.

   The coupon payment is recorded as interest income whether securities are held to maturity or available for sale.

16. B is correct.

   Unrealized gains and losses are included in income when securities are classified as held-for-trading securities. During 2009 there was an unrealized loss of €1,000.

17. C is correct.

   The difference between historical cost and par value must be amortized when securities are classified as held-to-maturity. If the par value is more than the initial cost the amortization increases interest income.

18. B is correct.

   Under IFRS, SPEs cannot be classified as "qualifying" and must be consolidated if they are conducted for the benefit of the sponsoring entity.

19. B is correct.

   Statewide Medical was accounted under the pooling of interest method, which causes all of Statewide's assets and liabilities to be reported at historical book value. The excess of assets over liabilities generally is lower using the historical book value method than using the fair value method (this latter method must be used under currently required purchase accounting). It would have no effect on revenue.

20. A is correct.

   Under U.S. GAAP, joint ventures should be accounted using the equity method, which records BetterCare's interest in the joint venture's net profit as a single line item, but shows no line-by-line contribution to sales or expenses.

21. B is correct.

   Under U.S. GAAP (equity method), BetterCare's operating income will not include a contribution from the joint venture. Under IFRS (proportionate consolidation), Supreme Healthcare will report its 50 percent share of the venture's operating income.

22. B is correct.

   Under the proportionate consolidation method, Supreme Healthcare's consolidated financial statements will include its 50 percent share of the joint venture's total assets.

23. C is correct.

   The choice of equity method or proportionate consolidation does not affect reported shareholders' equity.

24. B is correct.

   Selling receivables does not impact sales. It transfers a balance from accounts receivable to cash.

CHAPTER 16

MULTINATIONAL OPERATIONS

SOLUTIONS

1. B is correct.
   IAS 21 requires that the financial statements of the foreign entity first be restated for local inflation using the procedures outlined in IAS 29, "Financial Reporting in Hyperinflationary Economies." Then, the inflation-restated foreign currency financial statements are translated into the parent's presentation currency using the current exchange rate. Under U.S. GAAP the temporal method would be used with no restatement.

2. C is correct.
   Ruiza expects the EUR to appreciate against the UAH. Cost of sales will be lower and gross profit higher when the same number of euros will buy more inventory—in this case, later. The weighted average cost and current rate methods will provide the strongest euro translation rate for inventory.

3. B is correct.
   If the parent's currency is chosen as the functional currency the temporal method must be used. Under the temporal method, fixed assets are translated using the rate in effect at the time they were acquired.

4. C is correct.
   Monetary assets and liabilities such as accounts receivable are translated at current (end-of-period) rates regardless of whether the temporal or current rate method is being used.

5. B is correct.
   When the foreign currency is chosen as the functional currency, the current rate method is used. All assets and liabilities are translated at the current (end-of-period) rate.

6. B is correct.
   When the foreign currency is chosen as the functional currency the current rate method must be used and all gains or losses from translation are reported as a cumulative

translation adjustment to shareholder equity. When the foreign currency decreases in value (weakens), the current rate method results in a negative translation adjustment in stockholders' equity.

7. B is correct.
When the parent's currency is used as the functional currency, the temporal method must be used to translate the subsidiary's accounts. Under the temporal method, monetary assets and liabilities (e.g., debt) are translated at the current (year-end) rate, nonmonetary assets and liabilities measured at historical cost (e.g., inventory) are translated at historical exchange rates, and nonmonetary assets and liabilities measured at current value are translated at the exchange rate at the date when the current value was determined. Because beginning inventory was sold first and sales and purchases were evenly acquired, the average rate is most appropriate for translating inventory and $77 \times 0.92 = \$71$. Long-term debt is translated at the year-end rate of $0.95. $175 \times 0.95 = \$166$.

8. B is correct.
Translating the 2007 balance sheet using the temporal method, as is required here, results in assets of $370 million. The translated liabilities and common stock amount to $326 million, meaning that the value for 2007 retained earnings is: $370 million − $326 million = $44 million.

Account	Temporal Method (2007)		
	C$	Rate	US$
Cash	135	0.95	128
Accounts receivable	98	0.95	93
Inventory	77	0.92	71
Fixed assets	100	0.86	86
Accumulated depreciation	(10)	0.86	(9)
Total assets	400		370
Accounts payable	77	0.95	73
Long-term debt	175	0.95	166
Common stock	100	0.86	86
Retained earnings	48	To balance	44
Total liabilities and shareholders' equity	400		370

9. C is correct.
The Canadian dollar would be the appropriate reporting currency when substantially all operating, financing, and investing decisions are based on the local currency. The parent country's inflation rate is never relevant. Earnings manipulation is not justified, and at any rate changing the functional currency would take the gains off of the income statement.

10. C is correct.

    If the functional currency was changed from the parent currency (U.S. dollar) to the local currency (Canadian dollar), the current rate method would replace the temporal method. The temporal method ignores unrealized gains and losses on nonmonetary assets and liabilities, but the current rate method does not.

11. B is correct.

    If the Canadian currency is chosen as the functional currency the current rate method will be used and the current exchange rate will be the rate used to translate all assets and liabilities. Currently, only monetary assets and liabilities are translated at the current rate. Sales are translated at the average rate during the year under either method. Fixed assets are translated using the historical rate under the temporal method but would switch to current rates under the current rate method. Therefore, there will most likely be an effect on sales/fixed assets. Because the cash ratio involves only monetary assets and liabilities it is unaffected by the translation method. Receivables turnover pairs a monetary asset with sales and is thus also unaffected.

12. B is correct.

    If the functional currency were changed then Consol-Can would use the current rate method and the balance sheet exposure would be equal to net assets (total assets − total liabilities). In this case, $400 - 77 - 175 = 148$.

13. B is correct.

    Julius is using the current rate method, which is most appropriate when it is operating with a high degree of autonomy.

14. A is correct.

    If the current rate method is being used (as it is for Julius) the local currency (euro) is the functional currency. When the temporal method is being used (as it is for Augustus) the parent currency (U.S. dollar) is the functional currency.

15. C is correct.

    When the current rate method is being used, all currency gains and losses are recorded as a cumulative translation adjustment to shareholder equity.

16. C is correct.

    Under the current rate method, all assets are translated using the year-end 2008 (current) rate of \$1.61/€1.00. €2,300 × 1.61 = \$3,703.

17. A is correct.

    Under the current rate method, both sales and cost of goods sold would be translated at the 2008 average exchange rate. The ratio would be the same as reported under the euro. €2,300 − €1,400 = €900, €900/€2300 = 39.1 percent. Or, \$3,542 − \$2,156 = \$1,386, \$1,386/\$3,542 = 39.1 percent.

18. C is correct.

    Augustus is using the temporal method in conjunction with FIFO inventory accounting. If FIFO is used, ending inventory is assumed to be composed of the most recently acquired items and thus inventory will be translated at relatively recent exchange rates. To the extent that the average weight used to translate sales differs from the historical rate used to translate inventories, the gross margin will be distorted when translated into U.S. dollars.

19. C is correct.
    If the U.S. dollar is the functional currency the temporal method must be used. Revenues and receivables (monetary asset) would be the same under either accounting method. Inventory and fixed assets were purchased when the U.S. dollar was stronger, so at historical rates (temporal method), translated they would be lower. Identical revenues/ lower fixed assets would result in higher fixed asset turnover.

20. A is correct.
    If the U.S. dollar is the functional currency the temporal method must be used, and the balance sheet exposure will be the net *monetary* assets of $125 + 230 - 185 - 200 = -30$ or a net monetary liability of $30. This net monetary liability would be eliminated if fixed assets (non-monetary) were sold to increase cash. Issuing debt, either short term or long term, would increase the net monetary liability.

21. A is correct.
    Because the U.S. dollar has been consistently weakening against the Singapore dollar, cost of sales will be lower and gross profit higher when an earlier exchange rate is used to translate inventory, compared to using current exchange rates. If the Singapore dollar is the functional currency, current rates would be used. Therefore, the combination of the U.S. dollar (temporal method) and FIFO will result in the highest gross profit margin.

22. A is correct.
    Under the current rate method, revenue is translated at the average rate for the year, SGD4,800 × 0.662 = $3,178. Debt should be translated at the current rate, SGD200 × 0.671 = $134. Under the current rate method, Acceletron would have a net asset balance sheet exposure. Since the SGD has been strengthening against the USD, the translation adjustment would be positive rather than negative.

23. B is correct.
    Under the temporal method inventory and fixed assets would be translated using historic rates. Accounts receivable is a monetary asset and would be translated at year-end (current) rates. Fixed assets are found as $(1,000 × 0.568) + (640 × 0.606) = 956.

24. B is correct.
    The current exchange rate is $0.671/SGD. That rate would be used regardless of whether Acceletron uses the current rate or temporal method. $0.654 was the weighted average rate when inventory was acquired. That rate would be used if the company translated its statements under the temporal method, but not the current rate method. $0.588/SGD was the exchange rate in effect when long-term debt was issued. As a monetary liability, long-term debt is always translated using current exchange rates. Consequently, that rate is not applicable regardless of how Acceletron translates its financial statements.

CHAPTER 17

EVALUATING FINANCIAL REPORTING QUALITY

SOLUTIONS

1. A is correct.
   Because debt covenants typically mandate a certain level of financial performance, they can serve to *encourage*, rather than discourage earnings manipulation.

2. B is correct.
   Earnings quality is typically defined in terms of persistence and sustainability. By contrast, earnings may be manipulated to deliver steady growth. Conservatism in accounting choices may reduce the persistence of earnings as the accounting often reverts to the mean over time.

3. B is correct.
   Accrual accounting is based on the "matching principle" under which revenues and the associated expenses are recognized concurrently even when the cash flow timing may differ.

4. B is correct.
   Cash accounting does not rely on discretionary estimates but rather on actual cash flows. This may be either more or less conservative than accrual-based accounting.

5. B is correct.
   A is the balance sheet aggregate accrual measure, while C is the cash flow aggregate accrual measure.

6. A is correct.
   Net operating assets are (Assets − Cash and short-term investments) − (Liabilities − Total debt) or in Profile's case, $(97,250 − 14,000) − (87,000 − 50,000) = 46,250$ in 2007 and 40,800 in 2006. The accrual ratio in 2007 is the change in NOA divided by average NOA, or $(46,250 − 40,800)/((46,250 + 40,800)/2) = 5,450/43,525 = 12.5$ percent.

7. C is correct.
   The accrual ratio is $[NI − (CFO + CFI)]/NOA$ or $[14,000 − (17,300 − 12,400)]/39,000 = 9,100/39,000 = 23.3$ percent.

8. A is correct.
Sales = Cash collected from customers + Increase in accounts receivable − Increase in deferred revenue.

9. A is correct.
Reported sales results are affected by management's estimates of, among other things, uncollectible receivables, warranty costs, and returns.

10. A is correct.
Cash collected from customers equals sales minus the net increase in accounts receivable, plus the net increase in deferred revenue. Cash collected from customers = 14.3 billion sales − 0.7 billion increase in receivables + 0.5 billion increase in unearned revenue = €14.1 billion.

11. B is correct.
Revenue was increased by a $3 million accrual for the change in receivables and also by the $4 million reduction in deferred revenue. Accrual-basis earnings were therefore $7 million.

12. C is correct.
The allowance for doubtful accounts *excludes* items from reported revenue and accounts receivable. An increase in this account *reduces* the discretionary accrual related to the change in accounts receivable.

13. A is correct.
Deferred/unearned revenue represents cash collected from customers that will be recognized as revenue in the future. A decrease in this account means the revenue has been recognized. An unexpected decrease could signal accelerated revenue recognition.

14. A is correct.
Ending receivables should be adjusted to add the €2 million of securitized receivables. Then cash collections can be calculated as €137 − (5 + 2) = €130.

15. B is correct.
By increasing the residual value estimate, management would lower the total depreciation expense to be recognized over time.

16. B is correct.
A rise in inventory balances could suggest poor inventory management efficiency, or also that costs that should be recognized in cost of goods sold are being capitalized as inventory. It would not affect the revenue line.

17. C is correct.
PP&E growing at a faster rate than sales may indicate that expenses are being inappropriately capitalized.

18. C is correct.
An asset write-down *increases* expense in the current year, but reduces depreciation in future periods (and possibly indicates that depreciation was too low in prior periods).

19. B is correct.
    Core operating margin is (Sales − COGS − SGA)/Sales, or (93,000 − 24,500 − 32,400)/93,000 = 36,100/93,000 = 38.8%.

20. C is correct.
    Although COGS/Sales improved and SGA/Sales deteriorated, the total effect was no change. 17,140/42,340 = 40.5 percent and 18,854/46,574 = 40.5 percent.

21. C is correct.
    One way to spot misclassification of ordinary expenses is to look for spikes in the incidence of special items for companies that previously experienced decreasing core operating margin.

22. A is correct.
    Capital leases are treated as though the related asset were purchased and financed using debt.

23. B is correct.
    The future payments should be discounted to the present value at a rate approximating the company's cost to finance debt of a similar nature.

24. B is correct.
    Goodwill is charged to expense only if it becomes impaired.

25. C is correct.
    Stock-based acquisitions do not flow through the cash flow statement.

CFA
INSTITUTE
ABOUT THE CFA PROGRAM

The Chartered Financial Analyst® designation (CFA®) is a globally recognized standard of excellence for measuring the competence and integrity of investment professionals. To earn the CFA charter, candidates must successfully pass through the CFA Program, a global graduate-level self-study program that combines a broad curriculum with professional conduct requirements as preparation for a wide range of investment specialties.

Anchored by a practice-based curriculum, the CFA Program is focused on the knowledge identified by professionals as essential to the investment decision-making process. This body of knowledge maintains current relevance through a regular, extensive survey of practicing CFA charterholders across the globe. The curriculum covers 10 general topic areas, ranging from equity and fixed-income analysis to portfolio management to corporate finance, all with a heavy emphasis on the application of ethics in professional practice. Known for its rigor and breadth, the CFA Program curriculum highlights principles common to every market so that professionals who earn the CFA designation have a thoroughly global investment perspective and a profound understanding of the global marketplace.

www.cfainstitute.org

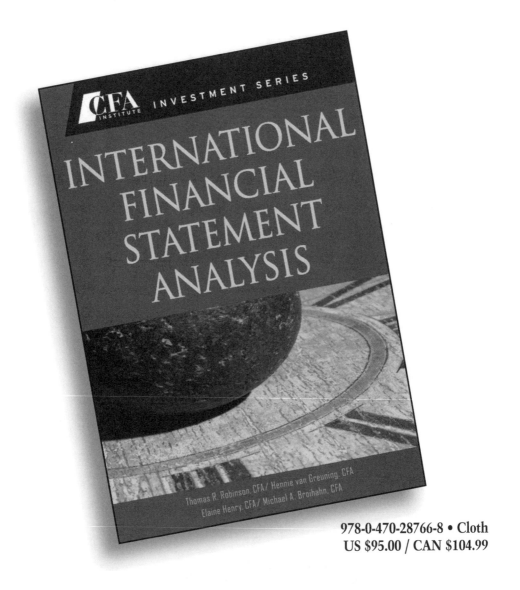

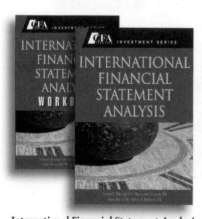
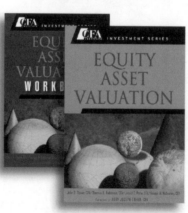